Ben Carlsen's
PERSONAL FINANCIAL SURVIVAL

A RESCUE PLAN

TIPS & STRATEGIES TO LIVE WELL AND PROSPER IN TIMES OF ECONOMIC TURMOIL.

From The Author of

BITES
of **NESS**
BUSINESS™
Improve Your Success Diet

PERSONAL
FINANCIAL SURVIVAL
A RESCUE PLAN

Tips & Strategies to Live Well & Prosper
In Times of Economic Turmoil.

Dr. Ben A. Carlsen, MBA.

PALM SPRINGS PUBLISHING
NEW YORK • MIAMI • LOS ANGELES

PERSONAL FINANCIAL SURVIVAL

A Rescue Plan

tips & strategies to live well and prosper in times of economic turmoil

www.personalfinancialsurvival.com
ISBN: 978-1-62050-608-0 (paperback)

Library of Congress Control Number: 2011922880
Carlsen, Ben A.
Personal Financial Survival: A Rescue Plan
Subject Code: 1) BUS050000   Business & Economics / Personal Finance – General

Published by: **Palm Springs Publishing**, Miami, FL, Los Angeles, CA, New York, NY
www.palmspringspublishing.com
Printed in USA

Disclaimer: This book is for educational purposes only. The publisher, and/or the author assume no liability for any financial losses or obligations which may result from following the advice, recommendations, or suggestions herein.
Financial actions entail risk, and poor choices may result in adverse consequences. Readers are advised to seek expert advice from attorneys, CPA's, Financial Planners, Tax law experts, Real Estate professionals, etc. before taking risks and/or making significant financial decisions.

Please note: Mention of specific companies, organizations or brands does not imply an endorsement by the author, and there is no fiduciary connection between the author or publisher with any of these organizations, services or products.

Cover design and graphics by: Rmada Concepts
www.RmadaConcepts.com

CONTENTS

Chapter Two –

Chapter Three –

Chapter Four –

Strategies and Tips for Solving Your Financial Problems

Chapter Five –

Choosing Financial Experts (by Krzysztof Bryniuk)

Chapter Six –

Exhibits –

"Greed is good!"

...Gordon Gekko in Wall Street

Foreword

It was my pleasure to provide this foreword, as I have met few people as dedicated and caring as the author - my long time friend, Ben Carlsen.

As many of you may be aware, the financial challenges of someone with debt may be incredible and at times over-whelming. Dr. Carlsen's book: *Personal Financial Survival: A Rescue Plan* addresses this issue and many more. Its purpose is to motivate you into taking action NOW! I truly believe knowledge is power, and in these pages you will gain knowledge and power!

Personal money management is a subject seldom taught in high school or college. As a successful businessman, I had to learn the hard way. Upon graduating from college I came home to find my mom's house was in foreclosure, and her car was about to be repossessed. When I asked my mom, "what are we going to do?" She said: "You're the one with the college degree; you figure it out." And, by using many of the strategies that you'll find in this book I was able to not only change my life - but the lives of many.

I am now President of *Professional Negotiators, Inc.*, a firm dedicated to helping people find their way out of oppres-sive debt, improve their credit, reduce or eliminate their obligations, manage their finances, and negotiate for bet-ter deals on major purchases.

My thousands of customers have enjoyed the relief and freedom that being in control of their personal finances brings. I wish you well in your efforts to do the same.

Plinio Vargas,

President,
Professional Negotiators, Inc.
Miami, Florida

PREFACE

First, a word about the title. The original working title for this book was "Personal Financial Survival in the 21st Century." However, I discovered that a Canadian author had written a book with a very similar title. I have nothing against Canadians or the 21st century, but I felt the title would be more compelling and reflective of the content if I substituted "A Rescue Plan" in lieu of "in the 21st Century."

Many would argue that their top priority is health, or family or religion. And, rightfully so. Although in our post-agrarian, primarily urban society you can't even put food on your table without money, let alone raise a family, or take care of your health needs. So your financial survival must be at the top of your priorities although it may share this position with other important values. And, if you're in trouble, you need a *Rescue Plan*.

Second, my primary purpose in writing this book is not to get you to think, but to motivate you to act! Of course in order to do that I have to stimulate your thinking.

Third, this book is intended to be alarming and encouraging at the same time. It is not a definitive review of all financial issues, regulations, instruments, strategies, or solutions. If you want that, buy a textbook on the subject. Instead, this is a straight-forward discussion of typical financial problems faced by individuals and families in this confusing period. And, an explanation of the most effective solutions.

Times are tough! How are you doing? Surviving or thriving? Optimistic or pessimistic?

As I watch my friends, colleagues, family members, students, neighbors and acquaintances juggle their checkbooks, I wonder. As I see them trying to hold onto their jobs, live on less income, pay their bills, and save their homes, I'm amazed, empathetic, and strangely optimistic. Most of us are trying to cling to a lifestyle that is obsolete. Circumstances have changed, and we need to change!

Perhaps small modifications to our lifestyle will suffice, but I suspect not. We're in an economic "sea change" and we need to act accordingly. "Rearranging the deck chairs on the Titanic" is a saying that comes to mind. It's a classic example of non-productive, silly activity when confronted with a crisis of epic proportions. Rearranging the deck chairs on your personal financial ship won't prevent it from sinking either. But at least you'll go down in style, comfortable and nice appearing until the very end.

If instead of waiting until the ship sinks you want to take proactive steps then this book is designed for you. It's a call to action: "Man the Lifeboats!"

ACKNOWLEDGMENTS

Many individuals contributed to the origin and publication of this book. Here are a few:

My parents, *Ben and Dorothy Carlsen* who tried to teach me financial responsibility, along with positive values and ethics.

My brother *Gary* who, although he's younger, is a role model for financial stability.

My nephews, *Greg, Jeff, and Darren* (and their families) who learned their work ethic and financial good-sense from their father, *Gary*; and my niece *Lisa*, and her brother *Scott* who learned their entrepreneurship from my sister *Arla*, and their father, *Bob*.

My friend, *Hendrick Ferguson*, who inspired me to write; and his company (Stanyard Creek Publishing) published my first book.

My friend, *Elsie Delva-Smith*, who stands by me with encouragement, support and consistently good advice.

My colleague and friend, *Krzysztof Bryniuk*, who authored Chapter Five.

My friend, Plinio Vargas; excellent adviser, superb negotiator, and a great person to consult for aggressive financial action.

My neighbor and friend, *Michael Broyard,* who has greatly assisted with the editing of both of my books.

And, my students, who educated me about financial strife and personal sacrifice for a better future.

In God we trust; all others must pay cash

Unknown

There are people who have money and people who are rich.

~Coco Chanel

He looks the whole world in the face for he owes not any man.

~Henry Wadsworth Longfellow

Money is better than poverty, if only for financial reasons.

~Woody Allen

I don't like money, actually, but it quiets my nerves.

~Joe Louis

INTRODUCTION

The world economy is in disarray, and in many ways the United States is, once again, the leader. This may not be the leadership role we want. We have the world's largest national debt, and a horrible trade balance. We're losing our productive capacity to foreign competition and along with it millions of jobs. Many of our states, counties and cities are broke, as are many of our citizens. Businesses are in trouble with some closing their doors forever.

What can we do to correct the situation? Well, while the "great economic minds" try to figure out ways to solve the macro problems, you need to look after yourself! This book is about helping yourself. Get out of debt, restructure your finances, and immunize your family against the financial chaos that surrounds them.

This book is organized as follows: Chapter One – *Financial Chaos*, provides background and context, and explains our complex relationship with money; Chapter Two – *Where Do I stand, Financially?*, provides you with the information and tools to assess your current financial situation; Chapter Three – *Financial Problems, and Deciding on a Strategy*, explores the major financial problems confronting most individuals and families, along with the pros and cons of taking action for each; Chapter Four – *Strategies and Tips for Solving Your Financial Problems*, gets down to the "nitty-gritty" of taking responsible, direct, and immediate actions to solve your problems and gain a stronger financial position, Chapter Five – *Choosing Financial Experts*, provides advice for getting expert help when necessary, and Chapter Six – *Conclusion*, ties up the loose ends and provides more motivation to take action.

By the time you've finished this book you will have a better understanding of why you, and so many others, have an unhealthy relationship with money and what you can do to correct it. You will understand what it takes to be responsible, make more money, save more, and become financially secure.

Conventional wisdom never is! Don't listen to the financial pundits, the investment bankers or the politicians. They all have their own agenda, and it may not be helpful to your financial security. Look after yourself. Get your financial house in order. And get started now.

Don't be immobilized by fear. Fear of unemployment, fear of poverty, fear of not being able to pay your bills, fear of losing your home, fear of bankruptcy... Your biggest fear should be INACTION. For if you become proactive you will feel better, make better decisions, and have the chance to solve your problems and "Live Well and Prosper in times of economic turmoil."

After all, who cares more about your finances than you? Does your family, friends, neighbors, bank, employer, church, or the government? Certainly not!

No, you're on your own! And you need knowledge and motivation. That's why I wrote this book and why you purchased it!

We live in a time of financial irresponsibility.

Dr. Ben

CHAPTER

1

FINANCIAL
CHAOS

The safe way to double your money is to fold it over once and put it in your pocket.

~Frank Hubbard

Credit buying is much like being drunk. The buzz happens immediately and gives you a lift....
The hangover comes the day after.

~Joyce Brothers

Another way to solve the traffic problems of this country is to pass a law that only paid-for cars be allowed to use the highways.

~Will Rogers

My problem lies in reconciling my gross habits with my net income.

~Errol Flynn

Strange Values

The United States of America was founded on principles and values that have served us well. The fundamental goals of *Life, Liberty, and the Pursuit of Happiness*, were supported by a value system which included a strong work ethic, and a pioneer (entrepreneurial) spirit. The additional values of thrift, family, community, principled behavior, and integrity provided an excellent framework for success. These values and characteristics, along with a capitalistic system and a territory filled with abundant resources gave us the opportunity for financial and personal achievement. And we collectively enjoyed remarkable progress and success for most of our national history.

Somewhere along the way we seemed to collectively forget our founding goals, values and principles. Instead, these were distorted into a grotesque concept of fulfillment. We became a nation of greedy, self-centered, consumer-driven drones seeking the almighty dollar practically at any cost. It began with the corporations and gradually extended to the majority of the populous. We didn't desire this money for security or charity, but instead we wanted "more toys." Evidence of this shift was the bumper stickers we began to see: "The One Who Dies With the Most Toys Wins!" and "I'm Spending my Children's Inheritance."

In the process we became debtors, because we never had enough money to buy enough things. So we borrowed, refinanced, charged, worked day and night, and decided not to have children. Then we could live the "American Dream" which essentially was based on more money and more stuff.

The Days of Easy Money

You may say; money was never easy! You'd be correct, of course, but we're taking about relativity. Compared with today, and the foreseeable future, money has been easy. At least it was easier than now. Government polices lubricated prosperity with ambitious homeownership goals and easy credit for home loans, a "full employment" policy, investor friendly tax laws, and an ever-expanding network of social safety-net programs. This stimulative economy, and buy on credit mentality combined with American manufacturing dominance, created an enviable standard of living, a dominant middle-class and general prosperity.

Unless you entered your productive years during the tail end of the twentieth century or entered the workforce in the twenty-first, you could, except for a few brief recessions, look forward to prosperity. Jobs were readily available, the economy was growing, your house was appreciating and you could count on making more money this year than last.

Winning the Money Game

How can you win when the rules keep changing? Time-tested assumptions and strategies that worked for much of the twentieth century are no longer valid or certain. For example:

--Retirement with a guaranteed pension
--Retirement at age 65
--A home is a good investment
--Having job security
--Easy to get a new job/career mobility
--Lots of jobs to choose from for new grads
--Predictable income
--Annual raises
--An ever improving standard of living
--A "buy and hold" strategy for investments
--Low cost food, gasoline, and other necessities
--Easy credit

If your mind is consumed with these obsolete concepts, you need to wake up. Things have changed. And the change has been rapid and profound. Face the reality. It's a new era with new challenges.

You need to change the way you play the money game because it's more competitive, the stakes are higher, and there are new rules.

Money is Good

Some people believe that "money is the root of all evil" - but it also is the source of much good. Money builds the churches, synagogues and mosques, hospitals, hospices, mental health clinics, and YMCA's. It funds heart, cancer, and HIV research. It buys food and shelter, transportation and entertainment. It funds your child's education.

So instead of "bad mouthing" riches, realize how much good it does. And although it can produce happiness or despair; in our society money is a necessity, a tool, an energy and a life force. You just need to figure out how to get more of it, and keep more of it!

The Family Secret

Most middle-class families don't talk much about money. The topic is generally more taboo than sex! Often it seems like bragging when you have considerable wealth. On the other hand, if you look prosperous but are not, you may not want to jeopardize your image.

And, many individuals and families practice poor money management, or make huge errors that they don't wish to divulge. Some have secret money vices, while others are just inept. Still others use money as a substitute for love, self-esteem, entertainment, or meaningfulness.

Various studies and reports have focused on the subject of *financial infidelity* (*GMAC, MSN Money, Harris Interactive*), and the prevalence of this behavior seems to be increasing significantly. Where a 2005 study showed 30% lied or concealed information about their spending, in 2008 it was 50%, and in 2010 80% of spouses admit to have committed this betrayal.

Yes, secrecy and money go hand in hand. When you don't feel comfortable discussing finances, problems are hidden and solutions harder to come by.

The Comparison Game

The comparison game is also in play when it comes to money. We've all heard the saying "Keeping up with the Joneses," and you may have visited neighborhoods where if one family gets a new car, suddenly there are several more in nearby driveways. If a friend or family member buys a boat, installs a pool, does a room addition or home remodel the pressure is on the others to do the same, or maybe even outdo them. And, if the next door neighbor is prettier than you, the temptation is to get a facelift, bust or butt job, liposuction, etc.

Of course appearances are deceiving, and the financial well-being of many individuals and families has suffered from the bigger is better syndrome, and the comparison game.

As we know, if you play you pay! With all of these pressures for conspicuous consumption colliding with the taboo on discussing finances people end up "living a lie."

The primary cause of divorce in the U.S. is financial problems. The biggest cause of depression, much crime, and social problems lies in a society where the primary value is $$$.

Chasing dollars for personal aggrandizement and appearances is a fool's game. Cultivating an "appearance of success" can lead to personal and financial failure.

It's Emotional!

It costs money to come into this world and money to leave it!

Even if you're a hard-nosed businessman, or a tough laborer, or a champion boxer – Money is emotional. I don't mean that the little paper rectangles in your wallet are crybabies or joyful; I mean the concept of money is emotional to us. We lose all sensibilities when it comes to cash! I'm sure you've seen people cry over money, laugh over cash, be depressed over their finances, elated to receive a check, or ecstatic to find a wad of cash. We've all experienced joy at receiving an unexpected windfall, and unhappiness over an unexpected expense.

According to psychologists people accumulate or spend money for an amazing range of reasons. For example: To increase self-esteem, gain acceptance, "feel good," meet security needs, control others, compensate for perceived deficiencies, overcome powerlessness, experience pleasure, manipulate people, "show off," displace energies, conform to social norms, demonstrate altruism, experience success, overcome depression, experience risk-taking and thrills, satisfy hoarding or accumulation desires, practice self-control, feel liberated, self-medicate, etc. Certainly money is emotional and can be a drug, a crutch, and a savior, or be used for it's primary purpose of meeting our basic needs.

For many of us our most dysfunctional relationship is not with our spouse, children, friends, or lover; it's with money! We abuse it and lose it, love it and leave it, covet it and reject it. We want to keep it close, yet push it away. We work hard to create a positive relationship but often our efforts end in frustration. And, unlike our spouse, we can't divorce it; it's a permanent relationship.

Yes, our relationship with money is emotional and dysfunctional. We need to practice "tough love" to change it.

Addiction

We may pity the poor addict, unable to control his compulsion to pursue drugs or booze or gambling, etc. But many more in our society are addicted to shopping and spending, and buying. And we need our "fix" to feel better so we go to the store or the mall and make unnecessary purchases without recognizing the self-destructive nature of this behavior. This addiction is so pervasive that approximately 70-80% of our economy is now consumer based. Remember after *"9-11"* when the *Bush* administration advised us to "go out and shop!"? Somehow it's supposed to be patriotic to spend, overspend, and go into debt. Don't buy into these ridiculous values, unless you're willing to sacrifice your future, and ultimately your freedom.

"Magic Thinking"

I'm sure you've seen people who manage their finances this way, and perhaps you have even practiced it. "Magic" thinking is when you believe some miracle or Santa Claus will come to your financial rescue. Just like children for whom the toys appear magically under the Christmas tree on December 25, many adults think that someone or something will provide money in their time of need. No need for financial planning, budget management, or material sacrifice, "it will all work out." God will provide. You will win the lottery, your great-uncle will leave you a substantial sum, the government will send a check, you'll get a raise, etc.

Well, they say "God helps those who help themselves." (By the way, it's not in the Bible but in Ben Franklin's *Poor Richards Almanac*, [although it appears that old Ben lifted it from an Alergon Syndey article in which appeared in 1698]). *www.brainyquote.com* However, whatever the source, it's still good advice.

Don't rely on "magic" thinking to come to the rescue. You're not a wizard, and your belief in magic won't solve your financial woes.

Living Large

Many of us enjoy the TV programs like *"Lifestyles of the Rich and Famous,"* the *"Millionaire," "Cribs," "Househunters,"* or many of the *Home Channel* series on home shopping or home remodeling.

When I go to the movies I practically drool over the beautiful homes (especially those most villains seem to inhabit), the luxury lifestyles, fancy cars, and exotic locales. It's escapism, but it leaves an impression. It makes you think. Perhaps if I were a "bad guy" I could live luxuriously. Maybe if I cheated just a little here and there I would accelerate my financial progress. These thoughts should rightfully be dismissed, but it seems as though many miscreants do quite nicely. When you think of the *Enron* guys or *Bernie Madoff* it makes your blood boil that these criminals made boatloads of money at their clients', and the public's, expense.

Of course you can make a comfortable, even substantial living if you work hard, save your money, open a business, or become a professional. However, as they say: "It's not how much you make, but how much you keep!"

Who's Richer?

Here's a question for you to ponder. Who is richer: 1) the fellow driving a Porsche, living in a condo on South Beach, and dining at a restaurant on Ocean Drive, or 2) the peasant in Nicaragua living in a shack, with a beat-up pickup truck, a horse and a cow?

Well, what's the answer? If you said the peasant, you may be right. If you said the South Beach guy, you may be wrong. You see appearances can be deceiving. The prosperous appearing South Beach guy may be renting the condo and leasing the car. Or he may own the condo but have a mortgage bigger than the value of the unit. The peasant rancher, on the other hand, owns everything he has, because he probably couldn't finance anything anyway. So in terms of net-worth the person with much less may have considerably more *real wealth*.

In Texas they call a person like our South Beach Friend: "Big hat, No Cattle!" In other words, a showoff without the resources to back it up. Many Americans have "big hats!"

It's all About Timing

Everything in your financial world has probably changed. And changed in a big way. If you're a property owner you've probably seen values go down; dramatically perhaps, depending on where you live.

If you bought gold a few years back you're undoubtedly pleased with its rapid appreciation.

If you drive a car you've been hammered with gasoline price increases.

And, if you're employed, especially in the private sector, you may feel anxiety about the stability of your job, if you're lucky enough to have one. Should you be among the ranks of the recently unemployed, I'll bet you're having a tough time finding another job.

If you're a business owner you may be wondering where all the customers have gone.

When you shop at the grocery store your eyes may have glazed over as you pondered the price increases of basic provisions. "Sticker shock" run amok. Advantageous for a few, and painful for most.

Yes, the 21st century started off with a bang! And indications are we can expect to see an even more exciting roller coaster ride.

Downward Mobility

This isn't the way it's supposed to work. We're all supposed to get richer and richer! Each generation should have a better lifestyle than their parents. When did the American Dream become a nightmare? Salaries for American workers peaked in 1997 and ever since then there's been a gradual decline in real wages and family income. On top of that, prices have been going up (admittedly at a slower rate since 2008), while investments in the Stock Market, bonds, CD's, have gone down.

The American family is being squeezed. Less income + higher expenses + lower investment returns + reduced or non-existent home equity + decreased job security = financial insecurity and misery for many.

The middle class has become the working class: Living paycheck to paycheck on a constant treadmill with no relief in sight. And with job layoffs, increases in living costs, and reduced upward mobility the working class has become poor.

I've Been There

I've been there! I've been a millionaire, and I've been broke a few times. I had a home in the hills of Los Angeles, with a swimming pool and a view all the way to the Pacific. And, there was a *Bentley*, a *Porsche*, and a *Mercedes* in the driveway. I had a getaway apartment in Mexico, lots of high quality art, frequent travel, and I never ate at home. In fact I ran a monthly tab at my favorite restaurant in Pasadena. When I wanted a change, I relocated to Florida where I purchased an even larger home on open Tampa Bay with a boat, dock, pool, *Jacuzzi*, and a *Corvette*, and *Mercedes* coupe in the garage. Then I moved to Miami, to a penthouse condo on Biscayne Bay.

Yes, it's fun to live large! There's no denying it. The problem was, I lived like I was rich, but I wasn't all that wealthy.

Although I had a substantial 401K, and an IRA, and money in the bank, I had mortgages, car loans, and credit cards.

In 2004, when I needed a triple coronary bypass operation I had the best doctors at one of the finest hospitals. That health crisis and the resulting six-figure medical bills combined with plummeting real estate values, the necessity to close my business, and substantial losses in the stock market, turned my financial world upside-down.

Poor Judgment

As we know, many people, even those with considerable resources, exercise poor judgment in their personal finances. There is a revealing article about the money problems of *NFL* football stars (Shelly Gigante, "*NFL Players Gone Broke*," CNBC.com, Jan. 31, 2011). Despite making millions of dollars in contracts and endorsements (sometimes hundreds of millions!), some estimates report "up to 80%," of *NFL* players "squander their fortune in the years immediately following their retirement." And, many don't even wait for retirement. In most cases "poor investment choices," are to blame, but "spending frivolously," "predatory" or "less than qualified" advisors (often family or friends) are a big factor. Some players blame their "risk-taking DNA," or "pressures to live a 'luxury lifestyle'," and "no free time to focus on finances." Notable in the list are: *Johnny Unitas, Martin Briscoe, Michael Vick, Deuce McAllister, and Raghib "Rocket" Ismail.*

I don't want to imply professional athletes are the only, or primary, examples of poor financial judgment, as there are high profile examples from every profession and industry.

The point is that everyone is capable, perhaps inclined to exercise poor financial judgment, and flawed decision-making when it comes to money (for all of the reasons discussed in this chapter and many more).

Resistance to Change

It's a challenge to live within your means. There are so many temptations, diversions, and options. Who doesn't want a comfortable lifestyle, an enjoyable retirement, vacations, a second home, new car, beautifully appointed living space, gourmet meals, a private school for the children, and all of the other accoutrements of prosperity? We all agree that "bigger is better," and that we *deserve* affluence in America. Well, we've been duped. Bigger isn't always better.

Warren Buffet is one of my financial heroes. Despite being one of the richest people in the world, for much of his adult life he drove an old car, and lived in a modest home in low cost Omaha, Nebraska. He ate at the local restaurant or fast-food outlets, and for all appearance was perfectly content. Here's a billionaire who could live anywhere he pleases, drive a mega-buck luxury automobile, dine in the finest restaurants, choosing to live well below the standard of many middle class Americans.

Most of us dislike change. We strive for a "comfort zone" where we can curl up and insulate ourselves from harsh realities. This is normal and self-protective, however, when the world changes you don't want to be a dinosaur. You need to adapt, and not at a glacial evolutionary pace. It's necessary to confront the situation, take action, and deal with the consequences.

Worst of all, you lose control when you're disempowered by outside influences. If you ignore financial difficulties they *will* catch up with you. Stop making your car payments and your car will be repossessed. Stop making your house payments and you're confronted with foreclosure and eviction. Stop paying your credit card bills and you're in store for scores of bill collector calls, some of which can be quite unpleasant.

The alternative to all of this is to recognize and accept your situation and take responsibility for correcting it.

Don't feel Ashamed

There's no shame in falling on hard times. Excessive debt, bankruptcy, foreclosure, repossessions, etc. are more commonplace than ever; late payments too. Let go of your *Puritan Ethic*, most of us weren't Puritans anyway. Forget the Biblical injunctions, or *Shakespeare's* admonition: "neither a borrower nor a lender be."

Look at corporations; they do it all the time. They delay accounts payable, renege on agreements, and declare strategic bankruptcies.

Check out the government. They're technically bankrupt, and *never* live within a budget. Of course, conveniently, they can print money whenever they choose, shifting their obligations to us peons.

Be proud of your debt. Obviously someone thought you were an upstanding citizen and was willing to take a chance on you and extend you credit.

It's nothing to be ashamed of. You're following the American way. But recognize that you'll feel a lot better and have greater security, more peace of mind and more options when you're on a sound financial footing, and have things under control.

Run Your Household Like a Business

Try to develop a business-like attitude towards household expenses. Your family is a micro-business, with income and expenses, products and services, goals and objectives. I'm not saying "fire your spouse or children" to cut costs. But you could try making them more cost-effective and productive. Instead of purchasing costly services from outside suppliers (outsourcing), arrange to have these services performed in house whenever possible. Some examples might include: car washes, lawn mowing, child care, gift wrapping, etc. Reduce costs as necessary by cutting expense accounts (allowances), supply costs (household expenses), maintenance, rent and utilities. Increase income by expanding your range of services and by value-added higher return investments and compensation. Invest in the future through education, ("staff" development), savings, additional revenue streams (e.g., part-time work or at home businesses), etc. Have regular "business meetings" with your family members/significant other(s) to evaluate your progress. Prepare written financial statements for the "Smith" (substitute your surname) enterprise.

Just adopting this mindset will help you reframe your personal and family finances, and focus attention on this critical area of life.

Motivation

A classic theory of human motivation is "Maslow's Hierarchy of Needs." Abraham Maslow tried to explain motivation by developing a pyramid with needs like food, air, sex and water at its base. Once those basic physiological needs are met, the individual moves up to security/safety needs, including shelter and protection. After that comes belongingness needs like family and relationships. Then come esteem needs such as achievement, status, reputation and responsibility. Finally, at the very top is self-actualization which includes personal growth and fulfillment.

Think about it. How many of these needs can you satisfy without money? Yes, air may be free, and possibly sex. But when you consider food and housing, and family and status, etc., how far up the pyramid can you move without financial resources, and how much can you achieve with these resources? Yes, it's your job to achieve financial security and progress.

Get Ready

Get ready to jump into an uncomfortable but productive process. In the following pages you will be asked to take a hard look at your finances. You'll be encouraged to ask some tough questions about your lifestyle. You will be confronted with some difficult choices and invited to take some courageous actions.

You've learned your good or bad financial habits over a lifetime. And, in most cases if you have serious money problems it didn't happen overnight. On the other hand, if you've exercised financial discipline and sound judgment, you may be feeling more secure. Hopefully, it's not an illusion because the general economic environment can always impact your specific personal situation.

In the final analysis, it's all on you. Your willingness to be serious about your financial situation, and your desire, determination and commitment to effect change, will determine the outcome.

In this book I've pointed out some of the most common financial problems, and spelled out some good strategies. The problem is, most of the solutions are painful. So, again, it's your life and your choices.

For some of you no action will be required. Lucky you! For others it will be minor tweaking. While for many, drastic, forceful and immediate actions are essential.

Don't adopt the government practice of spending your way out of debt. It won't work!

Besides, you can't (legally) print money.

Dr. Ben

CHAPTER

2

WHERE DO I STAND, FINANCIALLY?

BEN CARLSEN

The only reason a great many American families don't own an elephant is that they have never been offered an elephant for a dollar down and easy weekly payments.

~Mad Magazine

A bank is a place that will lend you money if you can prove that you don't need it.

~Bob Hope

Car sickness is the feeling you get when the monthly payment is due.

~ Anonymous

Know Where you Stand

They say ignorance is bliss. But when it comes to personal finances knowledge is definitely power.

When you watch *Suze Orman*, or *Dr. Phil*, or *Financial Makeovers* ---- you will see that many people have no idea what their financial situation is. Not the foggiest notion! How in the world can you get control of your finances when you have no budget, don't even know your net worth, your cash flow, how much you owe, or what your financial goals are? Of course, it's clear that you cannot get a handle on your finances, rein in your spending, and make financial progress without understanding your current situation. So the first step is to determine your standing. This means that you will need to create a personal or family budget. You will also need a "net worth" statement. But before we do that, let's play the *comparison game*.

How Much Does the Average Person Make?

The U.S. Trustee Program, http://www.justice.gov, can provide you with lots of useful information, for example, the *Census Bureau* Median Family Income by Family Size, and state or territory. Just for fun, here's a few, for single person households, as of November 1, 2010.

Puerto Rico..........$20,930
Mississippi............$32,131
Texas....................$37,528
Florida...................$39,383
Michigan..............$41,875
New York.............$45,548
Illinois..................$45,607
California..............$47,234
Virginia.................$49,484
Maryland.............$54,874
Source: U.S. Census Bureau

Go ahead, compare yourself! As you can see, there's considerable variation, and income is directly related to *cost of living*. How, did you do? Are you stacking up? Well before you start patting yourself on the back, or wringing your hands in despair, a few things should be taken into consideration.

If you live in a large city vs. a rural area the income, and the cost of living, can vary significantly.

According to the *U.S. Census Bureau* www.census.gov median household income in NYC was $55,980 (2008) in contrast to Watertown where it's $27,292. In San Francisco the median income (1999) was $55,221 whereas in Bakersfield it was $39,982.

Average U.S. Salaries

Now that we've looked at income by area, now let's see how your salary compares with other American households.

If you make over:

$50,000	you're in the top	50%
$100,000	"	25%
$200,000	"	5%

Source: *www.kipplinger.com*, 12/10

Where do the highest earners live? The states having the highest percentage of over $200,000 earners are, in descending order starting with the highest.---
D.C., Connecticut, New Jersey, Maryland, Massachusetts, California, Virginia, New York, Hawaii, Illinois, New Hampshire, Colorado, Washington, Texas, Minnesota...and then the rest.

If you're really curious (or nosy), and want to know home values, income and educational levels, and other demographic information for your city, neighborhood, etc. explore "Mapping America" / Interpreting Data at *www.nytimes.com*.

It's All Relative

It's all relative; if you live in Puerto Rico and have a $50,000 annual income you'll feel well-off, but if you move to San Francisco with that same income you'll be below average. If you make $50,000 a year but live conservatively you may have more disposable cash and more net worth than someone making triple that amount.

Remember: The median income increases with family size, although per capita income is much lower. In other words the larger the family, the more the income, although the increase is significantly less than proportional.

Debt

According to the *Wall Street Journal* (Mark Whitehouse, *"Americans Pare Debt,"* March 12, 2010), "debt amounts to $43,874 per U.S. resident." And, "at the end of 2009, the average U.S. resident's net worth...stood at $175,600." Don't worry if you don't measure up; this number is skewed by the obscene amount of wealth concentrated at the top. In fact, the top 1% of the population have an astounding 1/3 of all wealth, while the bottom 99% share the remaining 2/3. When you expand the view to encompass the top 10%, you'll be happy (or unhappy, as the case may be) to know that 70% of the total wealth of the country is held by those fortunate few. This means that 90% of the U.S. population is surviving on the remaining third.

Now that you know how you compare with others:

--in your locale
--in the country
...and how large the variations are between communities and states, and how much money is concentrated at the top, let's move on to your specific financial situation.

Two Key Numbers

There are two key numbers you should definitely know. If you've already done this, and know where you stand, you can skip these steps. However, if it's been a long time since you did these calculations you'd better recalculate. After all, real estate prices, equities values, etc. have substantially changed recently.

One number is your monthly cash flow that is determined by your income minus expenses. Use the *Budget* calculation for this. The other is your *Net Worth,* i.e., your assets minus your liabilities.

Your Budget

STEP 1 – On the page following this discussion is a sample budget form. Many of you have created one, at one time or another, but unfortunately most people do not follow their household budget, or keep it up-to-date. Please look over the budget, and notice the items which are included. These are typical categories for the average family or individual.

_____

Note: I confess, the forms provided on the following pages are not the forms I would prefer to see you use. These forms are samples only and they are useful in understanding the process and the specific categories which need to be included.

Unless you're one of those "rare birds" that do not have a computer, I highly recommend using the excellent tools available on the web. Some of these tools are quite sophisticated and interactive. Many will permit "modeling" based on various financial assumptions.

Microsoft Windows 7 also provides some excellent templates (*Word & Excel*) for household budgeting, financial planning, and net worth calculation.

So for now, just familiarize yourself with the basics: The calculations; the budget, expense, asset and liability categories, etc.

I'll have more suggestions for you as you read on...

PERSONAL FINANCIAL SURVIVAL

Monthly Budget

1)Gross Income
(Wages, social security, child support, rental income, etc.)
$_____
2)Deductions from income
(Taxes, Savings plans: 401K, 403B, IRA, medical ins., etc.)
$_____

3)Monthly Net Income
$_____

4)Expenses

$_____ Rent/Mortgage
$_____ Other home costs: insurance, taxes
$_____ Utilities: electric, gas, water, telephone, garbage
$_____ Home maintenance and repair
$_____ Transportation: car payment, bus/taxi charges
$_____ Vehicle other: gas, insurance, maintenance, etc.
$_____ Food: groceries, restaurants
$_____ Credit cards, loan payments, etc.
$_____ Clothes, dry cleaning, laundry fees
$_____ Education: tuition, books, loans, etc.
$_____ Child care: day care, after care, etc.
$_____ Entertainment: movies, cable tv, theatre, etc.
$_____ Hobbies, pet care, etc.
$_____ Savings
$_____ Other

5)Total Expenses
$_____

6)Balance (Total income less Total Expenses)
$_____

Instructions: subtract 2) from 1) to get 3) then add items under 4) to get 5) and finally 3) minus 5) to get 6).

BAC 12/10

51

I recommend that you go *now* to your computer and enter *www.Kipplinger.com/tools* where you will find a budget worksheet along with other financial tools. Or use the *Microsoft Windows* tools previously mentioned.

There are many free personal finance worksheets, calculators, tools, and resources on the web; find ones you like. The important thing is to perform the process.

Your Net Worth

STEP 2 – Determine your *Net Worth*. This calculation will determine if you're solvent. It answers the question: Is what you have worth more than what you owe?

A net worth statement is a "snapshot" of your financial condition. It adds up all of your financial holdings and subtracts your obligations (bills/debt). Remember that the market value of your assets will change, as many homeowners discovered in the current real estate crisis. That's why you should update your net worth statement at least annually.

Again, it's probably easiest to access the forms on your computer, then print them out, as it will be easier to work with these forms in 9 1/2 by 11 size. Be certain to be as accurate as possible. Where you need to estimate, like the value of your home or car, it's better to err on the conservative side.

Look over the categories on the following Net Worth worksheet. You may be pleased to see that you have more assets than you thought. On the other hand you may have considerable debt, as well. The balance is what is important.

———————————

Net Worth Statement

Assets

Cash on hand
$_____
Cash in Checking(s)
$_____
Cash in Savings Account(s)
$_____
Money Market Account(s)
$_____
Estimated Market Value of Your Home (check Zwillow.com)
$_____
Estimated Value of Household Items
$_____
Market Value of Other Real Estate
(i.e. investment or rental property, timeshare, vacation home)
$_____
Stocks
$_____
Bonds
$_____
Mutual Funds
$_____
Market Value of Vehicles (check www.edmunds.com)
$_____
Cash Value of Life Insurance
$_____
Current Value of 401(k), 403(b), etc. (employee sponsored plans)
$_____
Individual Retirement Account (IRA/Roth IRA)
$_____
Estimated Value of Personal Items (jewelry, collectibles, etc.)
$_____
Other Assets
$_____

Total Assets $_____ (add all above)

Net Worth Statement (continued)

Liabilities

Mortgage

$_____

Home Equity Loan or Line of Credit Balance

$_____

Other Real Estate Loans

$_____

Auto Loan or Lease

$_____

Credit Card Balances

$_____

Student Loans

$_____

Taxes owed

$_____

401 (k) Loan

$_____

Personal Unsecured Loans

$_____

Life Insurance Loans

$_____

Other Liabilities

$_____

$_____

Total Liabilities

$_____

NET WORTH (subtract Total Liabilities [above] from Total Assets [on prior page])

$_____

Analysis

Congratulations! If you completed these two steps I'm sure you're ahead of 80% of the American public. Examine your completed forms in detail. What do you see? Hopefully there's a positive cash flow so that you can have money left over each month. In any event, the Budget worksheet will help you develop a responsible Spending Plan.

Likewise, (on the Net Worth calculation) if you're worth more than you owe, you can breathe a sigh of relief. Although what may be most important is the trend. Is your Net Worth going up or down? If it's increasing that's good. If it's decreasing it's not necessarily bad, for example if you're retired and this is part of your plan.

Of course if these numbers look good, it doesn't mean that you can relax. Do you have a six month reserve of living expenses in case there's a job loss, family emergency, hospitalization, unexpected major expense, etc.?

What if the numbers look bad? If they're bad it's a *call to action.* You'd better do something right away.

I'm sure you realize that financial success and economic security are more of a mindset than an indication of work ethic or intelligence. And, our needs are more perception than reality. I know people with a $250,000 annual income who constantly "cry poverty," while others earning a fraction of this amount are happy, content and secure.

You need to examine yourself, your goals, aspirations and values. But of course, you need to deal with the reality of your present situation.

The first thing a financial planner, CPA, or other professional would ask you is: What are your expenses? It's easier to adjust your expenses than your income. Your income is pretty much fixed.

If you work for someone else you will receive a salary which is generally about the same each month. If you're retired, and on a fixed income you will definitely receive the same every month until there's a cost of living adjustment or some other modification. If your money is in *CD*'s or annuities or some other investment instrument it's also predictable. You get the idea.

As a part of the "comparison game" you may want to know how your expenses stack up against the average consumer. On the following page you will find a "detailed look into how the average U.S. consumer unit spends their annual paycheck."

Where Does the Money Go?

The Department of Labor's latest survey provides a detailed look into how the average U.S. consumer unit spends their annual paycheck.

U.S. CONSUMER UNIT EXPENDITURES
Average annual expenditures and percent of total

Source: Consumer Expenditures (U.S. Dept. of Labor, U.S. Bureau of Labor Statistics, April, 2009) as reported in *visualeconomics.com (October 2010 update)*

The characters on the chart are small so I will list a few of them for you. As you might expect, food, shelter and transportation are the big ones. Thirty-four percent on shelter (including furniture, supplies and utilities); almost 18% on transportation, and 12% on food (7% at home & 5% away). Other big expenses are insurance & pensions, at almost 11%, healthcare at close to 6% and entertainment at over 5%.

Less than 1% is spent on alcoholic beverages, and ¾ of 1% on tobacco; and smallest of all is reading, at two-tenths of 1%. Thank you for buying this book!

Your expenses can be variable, and are largely under your control. Sure you have expenses you can't easily reduce like your rent or mortgage payment. But you can alter transportation expenses, food expenditures, recreation costs, incidental and miscellaneous costs, etc. And, if your housing costs are too high, you can move to more affordable accommodations.

The Formula

The basic formula is a simple one:

In-Sp=Sa+Iv=A+R=Se+P

Income minus **Sp**ending=
Savings+**In**vestment=
Accumulation+ **R**eserve=
Security+**P**rogress

In other terms: Spend less than your income; this will allow you to save and invest, which in turn will result accumulation of money and enable creation of a reserve, and in the end will create security and progress in your life.

You Need A Plan

Without specific and realistic goals you may have a difficult time achieving the degree of financial independence and security you want. Consider your lifestyle ambitions and develop your goals accordingly. Some desire to own their home free-and-clear, others may want to travel, many want no bills, still others want a vacation home. For some $1 million in net worth may be essential, while others want a $5,000 per month income in retirement. For some a lavish lifestyle is essential, while others would be happy with minimal creature comforts. Whatever is important to you, you need to attach a dollar amount to it, and then back into the savings and income amounts necessary to attain it. You may want to develop your plan with a financial planner or CPA. Then you can test your assumptions, gain an expert, objective perspective, and increase your odds of attaining your "dream."

Time For Action

If it's so simple, why don't more people do better at money and financial management ? Well, I already provided you with many of these answers. It's a matter of understanding where you stand, recognizing the source(s) of the problem (emotions, societal values, living beyond your means, comparing yourself with others, lack of priorities and inadequate self-discipline, etc.) and taking corrective action. Now that you know where you stand, and why you may be in your current position, it's time to move on.

It should be apparent that a good beginning is to focus on the expense side of the ledger, and see what you can do. We'll examine some typical problems along with the pros and cons of addressing each one.

The next chapter will give you plenty of food for thought.

*The money Rules have changed
and your financial Game must change too!*

Dr. Ben

CHAPTER

3

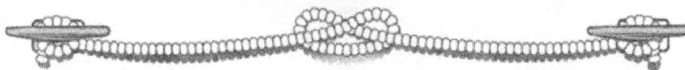

FINANCIAL PROBLEMS AND DECIDING ON A STRATEGY

I am opposed to millionaires, but it would be dangerous to offer me the position.

~Mark Twain

Empty pockets never held anyone back. Only empty heads and empty hearts can do that.

~Norman Vincent Peale

A rich man is nothing but a poor man with money.

~W.C. Fields

Poverty is the mother of crime.

~Marcus Aurelius

Confronting the Problem

After you've figured out where you stand you probably feel a little better. Even if you owe hundreds of thousands and only have $30 in your bank account just knowing the size of the problem is a giant step forward. And it's a motivator for change. *The bigger the problem, the greater the motivation for change.* As long as you don't "throw in the towel," thinking it's hopeless.

You've probably already considered some of the options, but you may not be aware of many of them, or of the consequences of each decision. In this chapter we'll explore some of the problem areas, and look at the pros and cons of taking responsible action in each of them.

Problem 1: You run out of money each month

Cash is King! Well, maybe it's not royalty, but it certainly can make you feel like royalty! Most Americans are addicted to credit. We *love* our credit cards! What freedom they provide. Even when we don't have money, we can still buy things. Who cares if you're broke? As long as you have credit you can still consume. The problem is our mind plays tricks on us. Buying with plastic is not the same as paying with cash. In fact, studies have shown that people tend to spend more when they pay with credit cards. It's not quite as real when you whip out the credit or debit card and swipe it at the checkout counter.

Many people don't even carry cash. They buy their clothes, gasoline, even food on credit. They go out to movies, the theater, restaurants, and take trips perhaps without a penny in their pocket or purse. What a life!

The credit card companies make you pay dearly for the privilege of advancing their money for your purchases. The *Credit Card Reform Act of 2009* did little to protect the credit card holder. In fact, most consumers now pay more. In anticipation of the restrictions on cancellations, late fees, more complete disclosures, higher minimum payments, etc., the credit card issuers raised the interest rates for millions of Americans. Interest rates typically increased from mid-single digits to low-to-mid double digits. Many consumers are now paying rates of 12-24%; some are even higher. To add insult to injury some of their credit lines have been frozen or reduced as well.

An obvious option to credit card mania is to go on a cash basis just like your grandparents did, or for the younger readers -- great-grandparents.

Credit cards are a relatively recent innovation. The first modern credit card was issued by *Diner's Club* in 1949. The concept certainly caught on. Today cardholders owe an average of $15,788 per household! And the average interest rate (APR) on a new credit card is a whopping 14.35%. (Source: *creditcard.com* /1/22/11)

With these high balances American consumers are up to their eyeballs in debt. And, making minimum payments they could spend half of their life paying off this debt.

The attraction of immediate gratification has seriously overwhelmed good judgment and left millions hopelessly in debt. If you take action in this area, and opt for a cash option, here are some considerations.

PROS:

--You will have a greater awareness of what you spend.

--It will help you avoid impulse purchases.

--You will be able to manage your money better.

--It feels good to have cash in your pocket or purse.

CONS:

--You might get robbed.

--You will feel like a pariah, because practically everyone you know has credit cards.

--You may have difficulty making airplane and hotel reservations.

So consider the **pros and cons** and decide if you're ready for the **solution to problem 1 – going on a cash basis**, and implement the necessary actions outlined in Chapter 4.

The "Dead Presidents" Speech

A friend of mine was one of the top automobile salesmen in the country. He made lots of money and attributed his motivation to "chasing dollars." At one point he became a sales manager, and tried to motivate his employees the only way he knew how. Now, I'm certain many others have tried this technique as well, and he didn't claim it was original. But he shared his "Dead Presidents" sales meeting speech with me once, and I never forgot it. In abbreviated form, it went something like this:

My friends are Dead Presidents. (At this point he would pull out a huge wad of $50 and $100 bills and show them to his audience.)

These are my best friends and I like to keep them close to me. They never ask me for anything but they stand ready to help me in times of need. If I want something they will help me get it. Whether it's a new car or a new house. If I get sick they will help me get treatment. If I have children they'll help me pay for their College education. Yes, my friends are Dead Presidents.

I will always cherish these friends and always try to have more just like them. And, you can be sure that if these friends were ever to leave me, some of my other friends might go too. Yes, my friends are Dead Presidents.

I suspect that you, too, might want to have Dead Presidents as friends. And, if you do, you need to work to get and keep them. So, go out there and sell cars!

by Randy Craig, Used Car Sales Manager, with permission

Problem 2: You're in Debt

Excessive debt is a terrible burden. It's like a heavy weight accompanying you 24 hours a day. Some people say they worry, can't sleep, get headaches, become temperamental, feel guilty, or discouraged, or have a sense of failure; hopelessness. Well, that doesn't sound like fun! So perhaps you should plan to move in the direction of becoming debt free. There are many ways to reduce debt or even eliminate it. Here are a few:

--Develop a comprehensive plan to liquidate your debt.

--Ask your creditors to reduce their interest rates.

--Never, ever, *ever* make only the minimum payments.

Yes, paying down your debt is a good option.

PROS:

--You may become financially stable.

--You'll shed many concerns and much anxiety.

CONS:

--It will take discipline and sacrifice.

--Change will not occur overnight – Be Patient!

Your solution to **Problem 2** is to – **Pay Down Your Debt** as outlined in Chapter 4.

Problem 3: Your lifestyle is too costly

Do you like to eat out? Me too. Enjoy buying new clothes?. Me too. Like to go out for an "evening on the town?" Me too. Want the latest gadgets; big flat screen TV, latest cell phone model, new furniture, maybe a motorcycle, and toys for the kids? How about magazine subscriptions, golf club memberships, or gourmet foods? You get the picture! Our *wants* are endless – our *needs* are few.

Living expenses is one of the most fertile areas for identifying savings. It generally provides more budgetary flexibility than the other categories. Caution: You may have to change your lifestyle! Your readiness to make hard decisions in this area will in large measure determine your financial progress.

PROS:

--You'll feel good when you get a bargain.

--You may enjoy the "money saving adventure."

--You'll free up cash for other expenses.

--You may discover you can live just as well or better – on less money.

CONS:

--Bad habits are difficult to break, so you will have to be strong.

--You may feel you prefer or need "brand names."

--You might feel "deprived," or that you won't win the "comparison game."

--Even minor sacrifices are too much for some people.

--It requires discipline and effort.

Is it time to consider **Solutions to problem 3,** in Chapter 4 **– Reduce Your Expenses?**

Tip: Marriage can be Expensive

Be careful in selecting your marriage partner. It's expensive to get married and usually far more expensive to get divorced. I know there's passion, "chemistry," attraction, and perhaps unmitigated lust is involved; but try to engage your brain for a moment when making this big decision. A good partner can contribute to your financial security and well-being.

Problem 4: You pay too much for housing

Buying a home is the single largest purchase most of us ever make. And, housing is the single largest monthly expenditure we have.

Most of us are not minimalists. I have a neighbor who lives in a ten by ten area of his home and rents out the rest. That would be difficult for me and I bet it would for you, too. I'm sure you've seen the tiny homes which are modular and could be moved conveniently to your lot. Not the most spacious, however, these are options.

The Rent/Buy decision is a major one. Some folks like the idea of home ownership despite the reality that less than twenty percent of Americans own their homes outright. Most of us live in homes that are mortgaged, sometimes to the hilt. This is an emotional decision more than a practical one. Set aside the emotion, and examine it rationally.

Your best option may be to sell your home. Particularly if it's an albatross hanging around your financial neck. However, there are many others. If you decide to stay put you may want to refinance. Loans, although difficult to get, currently have exceptionally low interest rates.

What if you can't sell your house? There are options here, too, that will be discussed in the following chapter.

PROS:

--Since this is generally the largest household expense, it has the greatest opportunity for major savings.

--Ability to take action in this area indicates a strong willingness to make significant change.

CONS:

--These are often the most difficult decisions.

--A home often has emotional attachment.

--If you move, it's the most visible and public change, particularly if you downsize.

Consider the pros and cons and find solutions to your problems in Chapter 4: **Reduce Your Housing Costs.**

Problem 5: You spend too much on transportation

Transportation costs are a big expense. In fact, it's typically the second largest expense (after housing) for most families and individuals. It doesn't matter whether you drive a car or use mass transportation, it's all expensive. We're one of the few countries in the world where there are almost as many automobiles as people. And most of us own a car or have access to one. It's the most costly and preferred option.

I bought my first car when I was sixteen. Did I *need* it? No. But, it made me feel like "big man" on the high school campus, and got me started on a love affair with cars. Many of you are probably the same. A car represents many things: mobility, freedom, status, independence, etc. Lots of families are two car households or even three or more.

Many of these cars are financed. So you're not only paying for gasoline, insurance, maintenance and repairs, car washes, perhaps garaging or parking fees, license tags, and depending on where you live, emission control inspections; you're also making principal and interest payments.

Insurance is another expense. Shop around for the best quotes and the lowest rates.

As with all other financial decisions there are tradeoffs. Here are some pros and cons of reducing your transportation costs.

PROS:

--Many changes in this area are easier. A car is more liquid; it can be bought, sold or traded in a large market.

--It is often the second-largest expense and has good potential for savings.

--You may rekindle the love with your old vehicle and not yearn for a new one.

--You may find advantages to public transportation.

CONS:

--You may not make the big impression with the newest, biggest, fastest, and prettiest car.

--maintenance of an older vehicle will require effort on your part.

--if you opt to carpool or use public transportation you may miss the freedom of your personal vehicle.

Consider your transportation expenses and find **Solutions for Problem 5: Reduce Your Transportation Costs** in Chapter 4.

Problem 6: You spend too much on entertainment & recreation

Entertainment and recreation are not frills. They're essential to reduce stress and lead a balanced life. You need to budget for these items and take the time to indulge. Your body will thank you and your brain will too! In European nations long vacations are the norm.   In fact, seven to eight weeks annually.

In the U.S. it's a different story. We're one of the hardest working countries on the planet. One fourth of employees have no vacation whatsoever, and the average number of paid vacation days is nine (David Moberg, "What Vacation Days?" *In These Times*, June 18, 2007).   And, it's even worse when it comes to paid sick leave with almost one-half of all private sector workers having none.

On this cheerful note, why should we even be discussing cutting back on expenses when there is so little free time for so many? Well, many people spend too much when they finally get to take some time off, and the entertainment component is the big one anyway.

Some pros and cons of reducing entertainment and recreation costs follow:

PROS:

--You will enjoy your vacation more if you don't have to worry about bills upon your return.

--You will free up more cash for necessities.

--You can substitute less costly diversions for the expensive ones.

--You may experience more family togetherness.

CONS:

--You may feel deprived.

--You won't have as many stories to tell your friends about the exotic places you've visited.

--You may think you deserve move vacations or diversions.

We all want more free time and more fun, and that's good. However, this may be the time to consider Chapter 4, **Solutions for Problem 6: Reduce your Entertainment and Vacation Costs.**

Problem 7: You're considering Bankruptcy

Bankruptcy should be considered as a *last* option. However, it's still an option! If you're buried under debt with no
practical way out, you may want to file a Chapter 13 or
even a Chapter 7. Chapter 13's are debt restructuring and
repayment plans under the supervision of the court, whereas Chapter 7's are outright liquidations where your
creditors get nothing, (with few exceptions).

Bankruptcy is intended to give you a "fresh start." It was
designed to sanctify the debt liquidation process under the
auspices of the *Federal Bankruptcy Court*. It sure beats the
"debtors prisons" that were the fate of some in much earlier times.

Think long and hard before you declare bankruptcy. The
Big "B" will stay on your credit record for years! It will
make it difficult, if not impossible to buy a home or get a
credit card. Although some people claim to get numerous
offers for credit immediately following a bankruptcy,
they're usually from sub-prime institutions with predatory
interest rates. The lenders know you're at their mercy,
and you're a good risk with no bills and the inability to declare bankruptcy for another seven to eight years (Chapter
7).

PROS:

--Bankruptcy is a really big change; an opportunity to free
yourself from much financial stress.

--You will have a "fresh start," a "new beginning."

--It will stop annoying calls or letters from creditors.

CONS:

--It's often a long, complicated legal process.

--It will destroy your credit rating for a number of years.

--It will be difficult (but not impossible) to borrow money—even if you need it.

--It is against many people's ethics, morals, or principles.

After giving thorough consideration to your financial situation, you may think the only realistic way out is: **Solutions for Problem 7** and perhaps **Declare Bankruptcy** as discussed in Chapter 4.

Problem 8: You don't have enough income or savings

Eight is a "lucky number" in China, and if you can save, consider yourself fortunate even if you're not Chinese. Obviously it's not all about downsizing, giving up things, being frugal (although frugality has a lot going for it), or perhaps even entertaining becoming a miser. That's not the message I want to offer. There are two sides to the financial coin (I like that phrase). The income part of the equation is equally, or more important than, the expense part. Think about it. Expenses cannot exceed income unless you're going into debt. So you have to have sufficient income to get anywhere.

Of course expenditures are more of a problem than income in our society. Most of us have sufficient income to support a comfortable lifestyle. The problem is we've become such gluttons, spendthrifts, and become so acquisitive that the *propensity to consume* (a nice economics term) may even be *greater* than the average family's income. But we don't want to overlook this important area.

Most people's largest source of income is their job. For most of our lives (if you're over thirty) this has been a stable, predictable, and adequate source. However, in recent years there has been economic turmoil which has eroded the value of this income and jeopardized its stability.

So many people have lost their jobs that millions have slipped down the economic scale, and been forced to rely on handouts, unemployment insurance and food stamps (do they still call them that now that they're plastic cards with American flags on them?). I guess it makes you feel patriotic when you stand in line at the grocery checkout line and proudly present your Red, White, and Blue "credit card." Not! But if it's necessary, why not get these benefits? Don't let false pride stand in your way. After all, you didn't create this economic mess (well maybe in an itsy bitsy way) so why should you suffer the brunt of the pain. You don't see the politicians and international conglomerate executives standing in the unemployment or welfare lines.

Currently, almost 10% of the workforce doesn't have a job. However, you would be wise to take the *Department of Labor*'s statistics with a grain of salt. They exclude so many categories, e.g., discouraged workers, full-time students, those who worked even one day in the previous two weeks, part-time employees, ill or disabled workers, those who can't afford child care (and therefore can't work), etc. The *real unemployment rate* is probably *twice* the *official* number – now that's scary!

My point is not to get you thoroughly discouraged but to make some obvious points: 1) Do everything you can to hold onto your job, 2) Full-time and part-time employment is less available than in the past.

Work isn't the only way to make $$$. Many frugal and/or disciplined people invest and save and forgo immediate pleasures to build a nest egg of security. There are lots of ways to do it, as you'll see in the next chapter.

Here are the pros and cons for **Problem 8: Increase Your Income and Savings.**

PROS:

--It's rewarding to save money or earn more.

--It will increase your family's security.

--More money = more options.

--You'll have more money for emergencies and fun.

--You may be able to retire earlier.

CONS:

--It takes effort, discipline and time.

--You may have to work harder or longer.

If you agree that the pros outweigh the cons, you should definitely consider: **Solutions to Problem 8,** and **Increase Your Income and Savings.** Read Chapter 4 for recommended actions.

Millionaires

The classic twenty-year study reported and analyzed in the popular book, *The Millionaire Next Door* (Stanley & Danko, Longstreet Press, 1996) revealed a number of "secrets" of America's wealthy. The surprising facts were that the wealthy are not that different than most of us. They just behave differently by practicing sound financial principles. Most importantly **they live below their means**.

In addition, the millionaires that were interviewed, focused on accumulation of wealth, chose their occupations (and spouses) well, and were extraordinarily disciplined.

CHAPTER

4

STRATEGIES AND TIPS FOR SOLVING YOUR FINANCIAL PROBLEMS

Every day I get up and look through the Forbes list of the richest people in America. If I'm not there, I go to work.

~Robert Orben

My old father used to have a saying: If you make a bad bargain, hug it all the tighter.

~Abraham Lincoln

Beware of little expenses; a small leak will sink a great ship.

~Benjamin Franklin

Now the Hard Part

Implementation is the toughest part of the process. Now that you know where you stand and have considered some options, this is where the "rubber meets the road." You will actually be required to do something. To take some action! Up until now, it's all been about thinking, intellectualizing, considering, exploring, evaluating, and planning. Now it's time to do it!

Chapter Four discusses many options to help you address the financial problem areas discussed in the previous chapter. As with anything of importance and merit it will require effort, discipline, and sacrifice. Prepare yourself to examine the following options and recommendations with an open mind and a predisposition to act!

Excuses

The more time you spend wallowing in your morass of financial difficulties and hopelessness the less opportunity for transformation and success. Stop complaining, quit being immobilized, cease envying those who are more successful and get your act together.

The first step is to take a look at your relationship with money. The problematic nature of this relationship was introduced in chapter one.

Change Your Relationship

Have you ever been in a bad relationship? A relationship that was unfulfilling, emotionally draining or hurtful? Have you been used, abused, or taken for granted. Fess up! Sure you have!

Well, bunkie, think about your relationship with money. Is it good, rewarding, happy, successful, productive, positive, committed, based on trust and respect?

Many people do not have a healthy relationship with: money...moola...cash...lucre...bread...coin...clams... pesos...bucks...dough...

Instead, it's often a strained one.

Treat money right and it will treat you right! Swallow your pride and apologize. Let go of your ego. Suck it up and start over.

Start by recognizing you truly need this relationship. You can't live without it. Repair your relationship and understand your areas of conflict. Do everything you can so it doesn't leave you. Treasure this relationship and you will be rewarded.

Good relationships are based on *respect*. Have respect for your money, and demonstrate that respect, otherwise, like a scorned lover, it will go away.

The suggestions, recommendations and options offered in this chapter are straight-forward and direct. As *Michael Finke*, Associate Professor of Personal Financial Planning at *Texas Tech University* says: "...complexity is really the enemy of good household financial decision-making." (*Ya-*

hoo! Finance, Claes Bell, "8 Rules of Thumb on Saving and Retirement," Jan. 31, 2011). I agree, and will endeavor to keep our discussion uncomplicated, and free of unnecessary jargon.

Managing a household budget is not "rocket science," but it does require a certain amount of knowledge and discipline. Likewise financial planning needs to be realistic and attainable. There is plenty of help available if you have questions or need assistance. Just be cautious in deciding in whom you will trust your financial future (see Chapter 5), and know that many people have done quite nicely with limited outside help. Ultimately, you are the one who must decide on options and strategies, and decide when and where to seek help.

On the following pages we will discuss some potential solutions to the problems identified in the previous chapter, along with a number of financial "Tips." Let's begin.

Solutions for Problem 1: – Go on a cash basis

Stop using credit cards! The convenience is great but the interest rates are outrageous. Try to pay the balances down, and eventually off. You're a fool if you make minimum payments; the credit card company will have you in debt for years, perhaps decades, or a lifetime.

If you have the guts, tear up your credit cards. At a minimum get rid of the ones having the highest interest rates. Usually that category includes department store cards, gasoline cards, and those issued by institutions specializing in "sub-prime" clientele. Say goodbye. Have a toast to all the good times you've enjoyed together. Then move on. It was fun while it lasted.

Tip: Use Cash!

Remember Cash? Remember those little green pieces of paper with pictures of famous Americans on them? Well, it's time to get reacquainted! Those plastic cards are no substitute for cold (except in Miami) hard (only if it's frozen) cash. Cash will bring home the reality of your spending. Credit cards often fool you into thinking you have money when you may not.

People who have practiced this cash approach suggest divvying up the amounts you have left after the mortgage, car payment and other bills are paid, and placing the amounts allocated to each category in envelopes. For example, one envelope would have your grocery money and would be labeled "Groceries." When the envelope is empty no more grocery shopping! The process teaches you budgeting, money management, self-discipline and impulse control.

Some readers have asked me if it's OK to have a Debit Card. After all, the money comes directly out of your bank account – no credit there. I would advise against carrying one if you have trouble controlling your spending. It's still plastic and not real money! And the inclination may be to overspend.

There is one more important consideration. Unfortunately, the method for calculating your credit score (*FICO*) takes open lines of credit into consideration, and weights the ratio of utilized credit to available credit heavily. So you may want to keep some credit cards and use them occasionally and sparingly for purchases so that they remain in good standing. This may prove challenging if you have *ICDS* (impulse control deficiency syndrome)-- although it's my term it sure sounds like an official diagnosis. If that's the case you might try locking them in the safety deposit box retrieving them a couple of times a year; dust them off and buy some items on credit. Just be sure to put the cards back, and pay off the balances completely within the billing cycle.

Tip: Credit Card Users Spend More!

Studies show that credit card users typically spend from 10%-18% more that those who pay with cash. *bankruptcy.com*

How will you pay your bills? You can't send cash to the mortgage company. True, unless they happen to have a branch down the street. So you will have to use checks, or better yet, your financial institution's secure on-line bill payment service.

Tip: Keep Track of ALL Your Expenses

Yes. Keep track of all your expenses on a daily basis. Give yourself an allowance and stick to it! Some people I know actually write down everything, down to the penny! Others monitor expenses of a dollar or more. You may be surprised at how much cash slips through your fingers each day. A money awareness is an essential step in managing your finances.

This method is not foolproof, if you run to the bank every time you run out of cash you'll defeat the whole purpose. Instead when you're out of cash, you're broke, can't buy – finito!

Tip: Keep a "Stash of Cash"

Just like chicken soup or "comfort food" having a little cash at your disposal will make you feel more secure, (and could be essential in an emergency or natural disaster). Keep at least a couple hundred around. Hide it.

People frequently demonstrate their disregard for money by actually throwing it away. How often have you seen people drop pennies, or even nickels and dimes on the floor and not even bother to reach down and pick them up. If you'll discard even small amounts of money it's indicative of a cavalier and uncaring attitude. Watch rich people; very few will leave accidentally dropped change on the floor, they will even pick up change dropped by others. Sometimes "newly rich" will let it lie, but frequently the newly rich don't stay wealthy permanently.

Tip: Pick Up Accidentally Dropped Coins

Not only will you have "found money," you'll be demonstrating respect. You may think it's silly, but it's symbolic and may be good Karma. Why take a chance?

Solutions for Problem 2 – Pay Down Your Debt

We discussed credit cards earlier. The high interest rates and over-usage are the major issues.

Ask your credit card company to reduce your interest rate. If you've been a good customer, aren't maxed out, typically carry a balance, and they feel you might transfer your balance to another card or pay off your debt, they may reduce your rate. Don't count on it and be persistent. If they think you're serious it's better than a possibility.

Many people have excessive debt and don't even realize it. As a guideline, total debt should amount to less than 35% of your income. Your mortgage payment should not be more than 25% of your income, and credit card payments shouldn't exceed 10%. These debt levels are considered "safe" but individual circumstances and tolerances vary. These days lots of folks have debt amounting to 50% or more and consider that "normal." Don't be one of them! Make every effort to pay down and manage your debt load.

Tip: Fe, Fi, Fo...FICO!

Watch your FICO score. This important number will generally determine whether you will get a loan, and how much
interest you will be charged. FICO stands for *Fair Issac Cor-
poration,* the company that designed the formulas to
calculate a measure of risk for banks and other financial institutions. This controversial measure of credit worthiness is
now used for many other purposes including employment
decisions. The score is based on your payment history, utili-
zation of credit, length of credit history, types of credit, legal
actions (foreclosures, bankruptcy, liens, judgments) and recent inquiries. A high score can save you 10's of thousands of
dollars in interest charges over the term of a home mortgage!
With FICO scores – the higher the better. The range is 300 to
850 with the median score in the low to mid 700's. Monitor
your score for free with an annual report from *annualcredi-
treport.com* (1-877-322-8228), or more frequently for no
cost at: *creditkarma.com* (a pro-consumer website that simu-
lates your *FICO* score and provides comparisons and advice).

*IMPORTANT: Sometimes there are errors in your credit re-
port. This can cost you dearly in terms of credit availability
and/or interest rates. If you find a mistake on your EQUIFAX,
EXPERIAN, or TRANSUNION report(s) immediately file a dis-
pute in writing with the appropriate credit reporting
company(ies). They have 30 days to investigate and make
corrections as required. (refer to Federal Trade Commission
guidelines at: www.ftc.gov/bcp/edu/pubs/consumer/credit)*

Have personal debts? Owe a finance company or bank?
Look at the interest rates, and if they're above 8% pay
them down ASAP. As a rule, you should pay off *secured*

debts first (so your creditor cannot repossess your property), then small debts, and then the ones with the highest interest rates. Why pay small debts early?

Because it will eliminate one obligation entirely, and give you a sense of accomplishment and progress.

I know, you want the extra money you're paying to the credit card companies to waste, have fun, or meet living expenses. Get a grip.

There is one area where it may be a good strategy to not pay off your debt. Student loans can generally be deferred – if you remain in school – or encounter a hardship. It may make sense to take advantage of this provision to continue your education and delay repayment until you can get higher paid employment.

Generally it's not a good idea to go to a debt negotiator or one of those firms that claim they'll reduce your balances by some huge percentage. They will often take your money and provide no relief. You can often do better on your own. Or with a reputable agency like *Consumer Credit Counselors.* Just remember they have somewhat of a "conflict of interest," as they're financed by the creditors, and their objective is to collect the money while keeping you solvent. They will also charge you a fee for their services. They can often, however, get interest charges reduced or even waived by many creditors.

Tip: Ask for Help

Don't be too proud to ask for help and advice when you're in debt. Ask your creditors to reduce rates and change terms, cut back your family spending, ask your financial advisor(s) to help you come up with a plan. And, if you're so inclined, ask for "help from above!"

They Don't Want to Talk with You!

Under normal circumstances your creditors don't want to talk with you, they just want your payments. Most have installed automated customer service systems where it almost takes a miracle to speak with a real live human. And the humans have been heavily scripted and have limited authority within well-defined guidelines. So if you're in financial trouble don't stress yourself out. Be persistent; don't give up. You may eventually be able to make arrangements. Ask to speak with a supervisor. Work your way up the "chain." You will have to make an effort to gain their attention, but you have something they want – your hard-earned money!

Tip: Check Your Bills and Statements

Perhaps you've noticed the error rate on utility bills (especially telephone), charge statements, etc. Most people pay little attention, and just like with the bar code system in stores, (see below) believe their bills will be accurate and correct. Not true (in either case). There are frequently errors. Charges you have not made, incorrect rates, extra fees, improper application of discounts, taxes, surcharges, etc.

Tip: Drastic Action

Occasionally survival means really drastic action, not just the changes discussed so far. If you're drowning in debt, and about to go under, you need an heroic rescue. When your survival is at stake, it may be "you" or "them;" and you must take care of #1.

You'll read about bankruptcy later in this chapter, but before that bankruptcy filing you might be completely upside-down budget-wise, unable to make ends meet, and/or have no real assets. People can get themselves into a real mess. If you're one of them, and have huge credit card debt you might just have to stop paying your creditors. Yes, as the saying goes, "You can't get blood out of a turnip." And you can't pay your bills if you don't have the money. Sure it will ruin your credit, and you will typically need access to credit, particularly if you are in the twenty to fifty-five age range. You'll probably want to purchase houses and cars, and without cash *or* credit worthiness you may be out of luck. But credit can be rebuilt and remedial actions taken. And, you can deal with your creditors later. Perhaps they'll have more incentive to negotiate better terms (on interest and or balance) with you when you're not paying them.

When the priority is SURVIVAL of you and your family, and you need money for immediate living expenses, the credit card companies will have to wait! Consider this extreme measure, perhaps consult with an expert, be aware of the consequences, but if it has to be done...do it!

Solutions for Problem 3 – Cut Living Expenses

Tear up your *Costco* card, *Sam's Club* or *BJ*'s card or other mega discounter memberships. Unless you're a business customer, own a restaurant or catering service, or have a large family, you probably buy too much, and spend too much. And stop eating out so much, it's not as healthy as home-prepared food and undoubtedly contributes to the obesity epidemic. Most of us are too fat, and I can speak from personal experience about the health dangers of fast-food.

Speaking of health, dump the gym membership. Yeah, I know it's positive and important to you, but you can exercise at home or in the park for free.

**Tip: Check Your Receipt
and Count Your Change**

Sometimes we become lazy and over-trusting. We think the computers can't be wrong and neither can the cashiers and check-out clerks. Wrong! Make sure you get what you paid for. Clerks may scan an item twice, make mistakes entering items, improperly count your change, etc., Items may be priced incorrectly, and, computers may not be programmed with the latest price reductions. Get in the habit of verification.

You would be shocked at how often I find mistakes in the amount of my bill, or the change I receive.

Addicted to buying clothes or shoes? Not every woman is a dictator's wife, but some still buy shoes like they are.

Clothes are nice, and we want to look stylish, but many people have closets full of garments rarely or never touched.

Tip: Don't "Shop 'til You Drop"

During the holiday shopping season of 2010, in the midst of the greatest economic downturn since the Great Depression, American consumers once again came through. "Black Friday" (the day after Thanksgiving) was huge, and so was "Cyber Monday," Internet shopping.

Don't feel obligated to save the economy, save yourself instead!

Reconsider your *need* for a jumbo flat screen TV, a home cappuccino machine, an upgraded computer, a new *iPhone* or *BlackBerry*, an intelligent super-size refrigerator, a new laptop, a professional gourmet chef double oven range, or whatever else your little heart desires.

Tip: Don't Chase Technology

Don't chase technology – you'll never catch up! That new Smartphone, plasma TV, laptop or other gizmo will soon be available at a lower price. Most technology is obsolete by the time it hits the market. Try to position yourself slightly behind the "cutting edge." You'll save a lot of money.

Bad Habits

Are you a smoker, a drinker, a gambler, addicted to porno, or maybe like to pick up a hooker now and then? Yes, I know it's repulsive, but I want to be candid.

The *American Cancer Society* says that smoking will cut twenty years off your life. So you're paying a lot, $4 - $7 or more a pack to shorten your lifespan. Sure, you enjoy it but STOP. Think of it only from a financial standpoint. Wouldn't that $150-$500 a month help your budget? Likewise with drinking. If you need help, consider *AA*. I've been known to have a drink now and then, and in my younger years a lot more than that. But I cut it out. Admittedly not for financial reasons, but nevertheless it's only an occasional vice now. Bar drinks are expensive, and so is drinking cases of beer or gallons of wine on the weekends.

As for gambling, I've known quite a few who squandered a small, and in one case large, fortune because of this compulsion. *Gamblers Anonymous* might help. As for the other compulsions/addictions gather your strength to reduce the urge or eliminate these activities. You can't afford it! Again, there are resources to help.

Tip: The Pawn Shop is Your Friend

Pawn Shops have a terrible reputation. They charge outrageously high interest rates, are in unsavory locations, and thrive on people's misfortune. But in a jam, the pawnshop can be a lifesaver. They will loan you money when the bank won't if you have sufficient collateral. No questions asked, no credit checks, and no lengthy applications. And it's fast – 10 minutes max! Of course, it will cost you dearly, perhaps 8-10% - a MONTH! This option is clearly one for dire emergencies, and short periods.

On the other side of the transaction, they're a great place to buy, especially for jewelry or electronics. Why pay top prices at jewelers or department stores. Yes, it's a limited selection but there are great deals. An acquaintance of mine wanted to purchase a video game for her son's birthday. Where did she go? The pawnshop - and paid a fraction of retail.

Here are some more tips to reduce your living expenses:

--Develop a comprehensive plan to liquidate your debt.

--Ask your creditors to reduce their interest rates.

--Never, ever, *ever* make only the minimum payments.

--Watch your bank balance – Never overdraw your account, the overdraft charges will "kill" you.

There are lots of other ways to reduce your expenses, here are a few:

--Eat at home vs. dining at restaurants.

--Buy only the supplies you need vs. hoarding extra stuff.

--Buy clothes on sale or at consignment shops vs. brand names at regular prices.

--Purchase "permanent press, "wrinkle free," or "wash & wear" clothing to avoid expensive dry cleaning bills.

--Purchase used furniture (from garage sales, *Craig's list,* second hand stores) vs. new.

--It's a pain, but clip coupons – you can save $$$. Expert coupon-clippers can save immense amounts.

--Watch movies at home on cable, rent movies, or get them free from the public library instead of purchasing expensive movie tickets and concessions at the cinema.

Tip: Don't Over-Tip

I've heard that the origin of the term "TIP" is a reward for good service, and actually is an abbreviation of "To Insure Promptness." Whatever the origin, don't over-tip, and definitely don't reward poor service!

Tip: Hobbies are a "Double Edge Sword"

Hobbies can be fulfilling but can also become costly obsessions. You've seen the *"Star Wars,"* or *"Spiderman"* fanatics in the media. They often travel thousands of miles and spend thousands of dollars to indulge their fantasies. I'm not knocking it if you can afford it. But hobbies can be rewarding and not overly expensive. You don't have to collect *Picasso*'s, *Lalique*, vintage automobiles, or rare antiques. The most popular collectibles are coins, stamps, dolls, and baseball cards. While high-end collectors may spend hundreds of thousands on these, more modest collectors can build a respectable collection, and experience considerable enjoyment for nominal expenditures.

Hobbies can also be turned into cash, or even a business. It may be difficult to part with your prized possessions, but many people do just that. And, you may have lost some interest in your hobby, wish to make some cash, or decide that you can sell things on *eBay*, at collector's conventions, or even open a *Internet* or physical store. There are many possibilities. I collect art (paintings and sculptures), I purchased a large collection in Los Angeles and when I moved to Florida I opened two art stores.

more...

--Buy appliances at Freight Damaged Stores or buy "open package" items - pick last year's model vs. the latest & greatest.

--Swallow your pride and visit Thrift Stores for many items.

--If you lack self-discipline avoid sales where you're likely to get caught up in the frenzy.

--Shop at low cost discounter supermarkets vs. high end, convenience stores, or gourmet stores.

--Make a list for *all* shopping trips.

--I've heard you shouldn't shop for groceries when you're hungry so eat up before you go to the supermarket.

Tip: Avoid Impulse Buying

Buying on impulse often leads to obtaining things you don't want or need, and/or not getting the best deal. Try counting to 393 before making a purchase decision that should allow you to calm down and think more rationally. If you give into temptation, don't be embarrassed to return impulse purchases.

---

more...

--Combine trips to reduce mileage and time.

--Pack a lunch for work or school.

--Make your own coffee vs. buying it at *Starbucks.*

--Have a garage sale and sell your extra stuff –
make money too!

Tip: Garage, Estate, and Yard Sales

These sales are great places to save money and get bargains. As they say "one man's trash is another man's treasure." You can find appliances, furniture, clothing, household essentials, etc. Someone paid full price for these items, but you won't. Go to the fancy areas to find the best stuff. When I lived in Los Angeles many of these sales had studio props, and new clothing with advertising for new release films. Hip, cool, and cheap!

---

more...

--Don't use vending machines for snack purchases.

--Purchase generic brands instead of name brands (frequently they're made by the big name-brand companies anyway – then private labeled!), everything from breakfast cereal to dog food, coffee, paper towels, clothing, laundry detergent, bottled water, etc., falls into this category.

--If using an ATM use your own bank instead of paying non-customer fees.

Tip: Cut Out the Storage Rental

Many people have bought so much stuff it won't fit into their home and/or garage, so they rent a storage unit. Frequently the monthly rental charges per sq ft are higher than apartment rent.

Suggestion: Give up the unit and cram everything into your home or garage. It will save you money, and you might be disinclined to buy even more stuff!

---

more...

--Disconnect your home phone (land line) and use your cell number (or eliminate the long distance call feature and use your cell for those calls).

--Consider Skype, magicJack, AOL, iCall, Vonage or other *VoIP* (voice over internet protocol) to make your calls.

--purchase your prescription drugs at a membership discounter like *Costco*'s, *Sam's Club, or BJ's* (the policy at most of these discounters is to allow non-members to purchase *prescription medication*).

--cut your kids' hair (the new styles don't require too much creativity anyway).

--cut your own hair, or visit a discount barber or salon.

Tip: Practice Defensive Shopping

Your shopping trip is not just a casual, enjoyable trip to the store or mall to pass time and purchase a few necessities. No, it's war!

Caution! Once you enter that store, restaurant or movie theatre you have entered a hyper-manipulative merchandising environment. Everything from the displays to the music, scents, product placement, appearance, color scheme, lighting, pricing, etc. is designed to get you to part with your money.

You are being manipulated big time! However most of us aren't consciously aware of these marketing tricks and strategies; all we know is we spend more than we planned to.

Be aware of these strategies and vow to steel yourself to resist them. If you don't want to be manipulated into transferring your cash into their registers: Go shopping with a plan and a list, spend as little time as possible in the store, and be conscious of retailer "tricks."

more…

--If you're "mature," shop on "senior discount" days, at stores that offer these considerations.

--Buy books from *Amazon.com* for discounts.

--Consider (inexpensive, or sometimes free) *eBook* versions for use with *Kindle* or other readers.

--Use tap water instead of bottled water (it's generally at least as pure and safe).

--Limit your restaurant meals (I have trouble with this one, but you may not).

--Hey, "big spender," don't think you always have to pick up the tab when you go out with friends.

Tip: Negotiate, Negotiate

Negotiate with everyone for everything – especially for "big ticket" items like automobiles, houses, etc. But don't stop there - even at Sears, Home Depot, etc., the manager frequently has some flexibility and will want to "make the sale." Try to get a better price from anyone who wants to do business with you, including: contractors, mechanics, repairmen, service providers, and professionals such as - doctors, dentists, and attorneys. DON'T PAY FULL PRICE or accept the first offer or estimate. You can almost always get a better price. And, it's fun to save money.

If you're not very good at it - practice, or seek help from an expert, or hire a professional negotiator.

Tip: Using Technology to Save Money

The technology explosion is a double-edged sword, it costs money to keep up with technology, but it can help you save $$$ too. There are new tech aids every day. Here are some examples:

Internet

Skype.com – make internet-based long distance and international calls for free

gasbuddy.com – helps you find the cheapest gas in your area

groupon.com – one of Oprah's favorites, shows deals in your area

SaveBenji.com – find good buys

Pricegrabber.com – comparison shopping for good deals

Yardsalemapper – find yard sales in your area

Yooza!! – comparison shopping

Social Networking tools

Facebook discounts – just type the item you're looking for in the address bar then add: / facebook

Smart Cellphone applications

Barcode readers; **Price Grabber, TheFind, ShopKick**

Yooza!! – mobile coupons

Shooger – deal mapper with directions

Coupon Shopper – allows checkout to scan barcode "coupons" off your cellphone

Expensetracker – to keep track of your spending

Tip: "You Get What You Pay For"

If you believe this, I've got a bridge in Brooklyn I'd like to sell you. Yes, technically you do get what you paid for. If you buy something you almost invariably get that something. That's the transaction. The exchange of money for goods or services. But most people think of this saying in terms of value. They often believe you get a superior product (or service) when you pay more: Cheap stuff = junk; expensive things = better quality. Unfortunately this is not the case. Shop for value. Get rid of that notion that higher cost means better quality or value. Take a look at *Consumer Reports*, frequently the best value is a mid-range or even low-cost product.

Although it may seem extensive, I've listed only a few possibilities on the preceding lists. I'm sure that you can find many more. Make it a game; see who in the family can come up with the most creative ways to save money. Have fun.

Solutions for Problem 4 – Reduce Your Housing Costs

Talk about a tough one. Housing decisions literally "Hit Home!"

Objectively review your housing expenses, and if they're too high you have to reduce your mortgage payments, your rent, your utilities, and/or insurance, whatever the case may be. Begin to like gardening because you'll probably be eliminating the yard service. And, if you can't reduce your housing costs enough, start packing, because you'll have to move. Maybe you'd be better off renting than owning. It certainly gives you more flexibility.

Tip: Get Estimates

Whenever you're confronted with major home repairs or remodeling be sure to get estimates. Prices for the same job can vary wildly, and contractors and craftsmen "pad" their estimates. Don't even take the low bidder, try and negotiate the price down further. If you're uncomfortable doing this; Fine. But get used to it.

Optional (avoidable) housing costs

Do you really *need* a professional chef double oven stove, an intelligent triple-door refrigerator or the like? Don't even think about remodeling, installing a swimming pool or re-doing your landscaping. The only exception would be if you have out-dated fixtures, etc., that need upgrading to sell or rent your property. And, even then go with quality, but not high-end items or projects.

Another caution: Avoid "Rent-to-buy" furniture purchases. The total cost will typically be 100-300% more than if you purchased the items outright. So if you recently moved to an unfurnished apartment fight the urge to have an instant "look." Better to save your money and buy used or new furniture as you can afford it.

Maintenance

Tip: Do Your Own Maintenance & Repair

Don't hire a gardener and pool man, do it yourself!
Instead of hiring a painter, plumber, or electrician, if it's not too risky or difficult, do it yourself. Get familiar with *Home Depot* and *Ace Hardware*!

Relocate

If you're in a high cost area like New York City, Los Angeles, Miami Beach, San Francisco, Seattle, Chicago, etc., consider moving to a lower cost area. Don't limit yourself to familiar places; a lower cost option might encompass a worldwide perspective.

Tip: Move Overseas

Think about leaving the country. Many retirees have done just that. If you're younger this may be impractical or out of the question. But consider everything. Your money still goes a lot further in many Latin American countries, some Caribbean islands, many Asian countries, and even some European nations (especially southern or eastern Europe). By moving to a foreign land you may actually improve your standard of living rather than scrimping by on less in the good 'ole U.S.A.

I visited Panama in 2010 and was amazed to find a modern country with American style infrastructure. Modern high rises, huge malls and shopping centers, great roadways and "dirt cheap" prices. I rented a hotel room for $35 a night, but found another that had rooms for $25! The bus fare was a quarter; taxi cab rides in Panama City $2-$4, breakfast at nice restaurants for $3-5 dollars, and dinner for $5-$15. I'm not recommending that you relocate to Panama. I'm just mentioning that it's very inexpensive with first-world amenities, and scads of Americans and those from other countries are moving and living there.

The world is your oyster! Or your home! Open up your mind to the possibilities. There are many considerations: family, friends, culture, language, moving costs, etc., and you may not even want to think about it. Fine. But it is an option.

Tip: Downsize (dramatically!)

An increasingly popular housing choice is tiny freestanding homes. One California builder advertises new houses from 65 to 837 square feet! (*tumbleweedhouses.com*)

Selling Your House

It's not as easy to sell a house as it has been for several decades. Prices are down; mortgage credit is difficult to secure. Over a trillion dollars in home equity evaporated from 2007 to 2010! Be cautious about making commitments to buy a home, and if you're the seller you may have to take a substantial "haircut." Buyers have many properties to choose from, most at very attractive prices. If you need to get out of your house, you will undoubtedly have to reduce the price, make the place stand out from others on the market, and perhaps offer other accommodations. Consider a "land contract" or "rent-to-buy" arrangement wherein a prospective buyer can avoid bank credit qualification, and a large down payment. Just be sure you have a responsible purchaser. It looks as though housing price decline may abate somewhat, but it's unlikely we'll see significant appreciation for years.

Foreclosure

Foreclosure is an unpleasant but sometimes ultimate recourse. If you can't pay your mortgage payments and can't negotiate a realistic modification with your lender, *and* you can't sell your house for what you owe on it you're a likely candidate for a "short sale" or foreclosure.

Tip: Confronting Foreclosure

If you've run out of options and money you may experience a the threat of foreclosure after about three months of missed house payments. It begins with the filing of a *Notice of Default* with the *County Recorder*. Following this there will be a *reinstatement period* offering you the opportunity to bring the loan current. If the default is not corrected, there will be a *Notice of Sale* and the property will go to auction. If bids are insufficient to pay off the outstanding loan balance the property will revert to the lender as an *REO* (Real Estate Owned) property. At some point following the foreclosure you will receive an *Eviction Notice* and will have to move out of your house. The entire process can take six months or longer to complete. In fact, in the states of New York, Maryland and Florida, homes don't "go into foreclosure" for an average of almost one year. And in California it's even more: "367 days." (*Miami Herald*, "Pace of Foreclosures 'Flabbergasting,'" December 31, 2010.)

Note: If you fight the foreclosure in the courts who knows how long it might take, or if it will even happen! The banks in many cases cannot produce the original note, have committed fraud, don't own the loan, or have already been paid. Get an attorney!

With the major decline in real estate prices, we hear more about "strategic foreclosures." Using foreclosure as a strategy to reduce debt, get out of debt, and exit a property that's "upside down" (you owe more than the property is worth) is gaining in popularity.

Refinance

Refinancing your mortgage is an option; take advantage of the low interest rates available now. Of course credit requirements are much more stringent than during the housing mania of the 90's. Just beware of points and closing costs, along with legal fees and taxes associated with these transactions. Make sure you plan to stay in your home long enough to go past the break-even point. Look at the numbers and calculate if it is worth it.

Tip: A Reverse Mortgage may Fast Forward Your Life

If you're 62 or older and have equity in your home, you may want to consider a *"Reverse Mortgage."* The plan is offered through the *FHA* and is technically termed *HEMC* or *Home Equity Conversion Mortgage*. If you qualify, instead of paying the mortgage each month you can receive a payment to help with your living expenses. This could be a very smart move. In fact, seniors who opted for this plan several years ago got more money out of their houses than the property is now worth because of declining property values. How pleasant to have your house pay you!

Tip: Reconsider Your Second Home

For most of us, it is difficult enough to maintain one house. If you have a second home/vacation home/timeshare run the numbers to see if you can afford it. Some can. Most cannot!

To summarize - Possibilities for checking housing expenses include: Reducing maintenance and insurance expenses, selling your home and moving to a less costly one, moving overseas, renting vs. buying or vice-versa, negotiating a loan modification such as a reduction in your payment, or forgiveness for part of your mortgage balance or a "short sale" if the lender agrees to your selling the house for less than you owe, (just be aware of potential tax consequences), getting a reverse mortgage, allowing your house to go into foreclosure, and/or fighting a foreclosure process. If you own a second home either make it pay for itself by renting it out or make sure you you can afford it. You could undoubtedly invest the financial resources that would be freed up by disposing of a "non-performing asset."

Also, try reducing your utility costs by raising or lowering your thermostat depending on your willingness to sacrifice a little comfort, etc. And avoid unnecessary upgrades.

Your home may be your "castle" but don't get stuck in it. If you can get by with reducing the costs, OK. If you need to move, face it and do it!

Solutions for Problem 5 – Cut Transportation Costs

People purchase automobiles for many reasons, not the least of which is to suit their image. When you drive up in your snazzy "ego-mobile," yes people will look, and talk. Perhaps they'll think "what a successful guy," on the other hand they may think "what a fool!" Sure, they may be envious, although they could feel self-satisfied and smart, because they didn't yield to the advertising and false societal values. *(With my love of automobiles, I'm the perfect sucker. However, fortunately I care more about the make and model of a car, rather than the year.)*

Of course you need to get to work, to the doctor, to friends and family, the grocery store, etc. But do you need a big gas guzzling SUV, a luxury car, or a new vehicle? Of course not! Cars depreciate at an outrageous rate. They say when you drive a new car off the lot you've already lost $1,000 or more in value. Ridiculous!

With new cars costing anywhere from around $10,000 (*Hyundai Accent*) to $450,000 (*Rolls Royce Phantom*) you have a large range to choose from. However, in almost all cases a used car is a better and cheaper option. The exception can be if you have excellent credit and qualify for a zero, or very low, interest rate.

When buying a used vehicle you're better off paying cash.

If you can't pay cash you may not get the attractive terms offered on new cars, but you should still come out ahead.

What about dependability? You will undoubtedly want to check the dependability of your car at *www.jdpower.com*. I also recommend taking your used car to a mechanic, prior to signing on the dotted line. And be sure to spring for the $35 to get a *CarFax* report (*www.carfax.com*) so that you can determine the history of the vehicle. Try purchasing from a private party to avoid the car lot overhead. Make sure you get clear title and go to the *DMV (Department of Motor Vehicles)* with the seller. Whatever you do, don't pay first and *hope* that the vehicle *Title of Ownership* is OK.

If you decide to purchase from a car lot or dealer, be sure to take precautions. Sometimes these are high pressure or manipulative situations. Don't be pressured into signing anything until you've had a chance to think it over. Generally, you will find that the salesman will present your offer to the manager, who will reject it and make a counteroffer. In many instances this is merely a ploy designed to get you to part with more $$$.

They don't want you to walk away – so you might do just that. When you do they will often ask you to come back for a better price.

Tip: Vehicle Financing

--Pay cash whenever possible.

--Never finance a vehicle for longer than the expected useful life. Keep the length of the contact as short as possible.

--Make as large a down payment as possible.

--Generally you should not use dealer financing; with few exceptions (like the zero interest option) it costs more. Instead shop around; use a Credit Union, bank, or other sources.

--Purchase the extended warranty outside the dealer; it's generally cheaper - just make sure it's an established and reputable firm.

I've bought many used cars in my life, a few were "lemons" but most were serviceable and a good deal. My current car is a used 1998 *Mercedes 230C* that I bought for less than $3,000! It runs great, gets around 30mpg (it's a four cylinder engine) and still looks good (see photo below).

Tip: Buy a Used Car

Frequently people will say: "I don't want to buy someone else's problem." But think about it. What if you're buying someone else's pampered "baby"? People sell their cars for any number of reasons and a problem vehicle is not the usual cause.

Gasoline is a big expense, and with the rise in prices you need to watch prices, and try to conserve fuel. Avoid "jack rabbit" starts, excessive speed, and keep tires properly inflated. Find the lowest cost stations in your neighborhood, and patronize them. Don't worry about brand names. Some stations offer a discount for cash. Use it.

Tip: Your Car Won't Care

Your car won't care if you buy *Chevron, Texaco,* or *Shell.* Generally petroleum distillates come from the same refineries anyway, although there may be some mysterious additives included by the time it arrives at your friendly neighborhood gas station. Also most newer cars will run just fine on "Regular," "Unleaded," (87 octane).

Believe it or not there are still good deals on automobile insurance. You just need to shop around. Don't get fooled by misplaced company or agent "allegiance." They'll raise your rates or cut you loose in a "New York minute" if you become a greater risk or don't fit with their demographics.

Tip: Reduce Insurance Rates

I recently transferred my policy from a major carrier to *GEICO* and saved over 30%. This is not a plug for that company as there are other internet based firms that can also provide a lower cost policy than your typical full-service agent or traditional insurance company. Look at your policy and get some quotes.

Repairs

Dealerships are notoriously expensive places to service automobiles unless you're under warranty with minimal or no charges to you. I call them "replacement artists" because they usually just replace defective or malfunctioning parts. Better to find a local independent repair shop. A good mechanic will actually repair problems in a creative fashion.

Tip: Get a good mechanic...

And treat him (or her) right! A smart, honest, experienced mechanic will get to know your car and keep it running for many miles.

It's a good practice to ask neighbors or friends for a recommendation or referral. Some independents are unscrupulous and will "rip you off," while others are excellent mechanics who have reasonable prices. Look for *ASE* certification. Car owners can save by buying used or rebuilt parts, particularly to repair a major failure. For example a junkyard engine or transmission can often be secured at a fraction of the cost of a new or rebuilt one.

Tip: Don't Buy Expensive Original Replacement Parts

Sure original manufacturer's parts are the best, but "after market" parts from reliable manufacturers, and rebuilt parts from quality sources, can save you a bundle.

If you have a major automobile breakdown be sure to get several estimates. I once got a quote for transmission repair of over $3,000. My mechanic fixed it for a couple of hundred dollars; all it needed was a transmission fluid and filter change, and new transmission mounts.

There are many other costs are associated with cars. You have to park them and sometimes pay for the privilege. Better to walk a few blocks, burn calories, and save your money.

Some people regularly take their car to the car wash, while others clean theirs at home. You should do the latter. (Or at least patronize the kids' fund-raising car washes.)

Tip: Electronic Components

Prices for "sensors" and other electronic components can vary wildly. At an auto parts store an airflow, transmission, or exhaust sensor may cost: 1, 2, or 300 dollars. First, many can be cleaned with alcohol, and last a number of years longer. Second, check the internet for your sensor: often-times the on-line supplier may have an after-market (not the factory brand) or rebuilt part for $50-$80. This could be a big savings. (Also, check ads for all other parts or necessities like tires.)

Carpooling

Another option in reducing transportation costs is to car-pool whenever possible. Often friends will each drive to a gathering, and employees who live in the same area will commute separately. Ask your friends and co-workers if they would like to ride together. Just don't end up being the sole driver unless others chip in for the gas.

Solutions for Problem 6 – Cut Entertainment and Recreation Costs

Movies are costly

A night at the "flicks" might cost a bundle. Tickets are around ten bucks, and a little bag of popcorn that has 20 cents worth of ingredients might be five dollars. A soda pop that costs a few pennies to make will typically cost several dollars. If you want to go (*I love movies!*) attend a matinee, use available discounts (seniors, students, etc.) and an affinity or discount card whenever possible. And, although I can't recommend smuggling in snacks, many people do just that.

Also, you should be aware that *Netflix* offers a service where they will provide an unlimited number of videos to your home for a fixed monthly price (currently $7.99 over the Internet, and $2 more by mail *[12/10]*). (*Amazon.com* is initiating a competing service.) Or your local library may offer an even better deal – free!

The Lottery

A word about playing the lottery for fun and recreation. This may be a shock in a book on personal finance, but I'm not opposed to placing small wagers, like one or two dollars a week. Just don't get carried away, and don't be disappointed when you don't win, because you won't! Alright, there's the slimmest of odds that you might win, but with odds of millions to one against you, it will probably be a free ticket or a few dollars max. The point is you get a chance to dream, and somebody will win at some point, and that somebody could theoretically be you. So indulge yourself, and dream on.

Vacations

Vacations are great and travel is wonderful, but you can easily overspend. If you like cruises there are excellent values. For $50-$100 per day you can live like a King, with room, unlimited food, entertainment, and exotic locales included in the package. If you want to take a chance, some travelers show up a short time before departure and if there are no-shows you may be allowed on board at a deep discount. (Although I understand that for security reasons this practice may be coming to an end.)

Tip: Airfare and Lodging

Because of fuel cost increases and cutbacks in the number of flights, air travel has been gradually been getting pricier. Additional fees including baggage charges, fuel surcharges, and security tariffs, along with charges for food and drink have also elevated costs. Some airlines have clubs which offer flights at ridiculously low prices; some are even $9! If you have a flexible schedule this might work for you.

Choose a discount airline like *Southwest, JetBlue,* or *Spirit.* Generally their airfare should be considerably less than the major carriers, however, this isn't always the case. Check with sites like *kayak.com, CheapoAir.com, or AirfareWatchdog.com* to get the best deals. Airfares are constantly changing, by the day, hour and even minute, so check frequently, (especially late on Tuesday's and early Wednesdays -when many airlines release their deepest discounts).

Be sure to get your "frequent flier miles," any upgrades, and other "perks."

Upscale lodging might be your preference, but don't rule out "home swaps," 2nd tier hotels, hostels, etc. Try *priceline.com* and get a bargain - the catch is you won't know where you're staying until after you make the reservation. *Hotels.com* is another good resource.

Package deals are not always the cheapest, but occasionally they are. The point is – do your research!

Be creative in your vacation planning. The elaborate vacations with 5 star hotels and fancy restaurants shouldn't be on your agenda unless you're really rich and not just think you are!

Tip: Wild Vacations

National and State Parks are great opportunities for economical vacations. Depending on where you live, there are really some amazing places, for example included in the federal park system are:

Yellowstone (ID)(MT), *Crater Lake* (OR), *Everglades* (FL), *Gettysburg* (PA), *Mount Rainier* (WA), *Hawaii Volcanoes*, *Grand Canyon* (AZ), *Smoky Mountains* (NC)(TN), *Glacier Bay* (AK), *Sequoia* (CA), *Yosemite* (CA), *Carlsbad Caverns* (NM), *Zion* (UT).

If I failed to mention your favorite, please excuse me.

Many people overspend on other recreational activities like video games, sky diving, motorcycling, deep sea diving, bar hopping, etc. These costs can be significantly reduced by limiting the frequency, looking for bargains, etc.

Just being cognizant of how much you're spending in these areas might change your behaviors and reduce your costs.

Squeeze George till he yells!

Solutions for Problem 7 – The Big "B"

The Bankruptcy Reform Act of 2005 is also known as the *Bankruptcy Abuse and Consumer Protection Act*; this gives you a clue as to its intent and focus. The bill was created as a response to financial and banking industry lobbyists who wanted to make it harder for individuals to wipe out their debts.

There are lots of misconceptions about the revised law. It does not prevent you from declaring bankruptcy, or keeping your home or car. But it does provide for a "means test" to determine if you qualify.

Tip: The Big "B" May be your Solution!

Perhaps you're in deep debt, behind in your bills, and can't keep up. Bankruptcy may be your best option. Don't let "false pride" or moral concerns stand in your way. Get legal advice to see if this is the best approach. Big companies and *Donald Trump* do it all the time! Frequently it's the smartest action. And you can start out with a clean financial slate.

Tip: Choosing Your Poison

Chapter 7 bankruptcies are called "straight bankruptcies" or "liquidations." Essentially, if you qualify, you're under the protection of the court. You may stop making unsecured debt payments (except on exempt items you wish to keep) and in a couple of months your debt will be wiped out. Typically you may choose to keep your house and car, other living necessities, etc.

Chapter 13 is designed for those who can afford to pay much of their debt, have substantial non-exempt property, wish to keep their possessions, and/or feel a moral obligation to repay a portion, or all, of their debt.

Some states are "creditor friendly, whereas others are "debtor friendly." Obviously, it's advantageous to declare bankruptcy in a consumer friendly state as you will have greater protection, and higher asset exemptions. According to the *American Bankruptcy Institute* the top five states most favorable for filing bankruptcy are:

1. Texas
2. Florida
3. Kansas
4. Iowa
5. Massachusetts

If you have lots of money you may want to pull an *"O.J."* and move to Florida. Remember, bankruptcy is a major decision and you need competent legal advice. Don't go to the local stationery store and buy a "do it yourself kit"!

Solutions for Problem 8 – Increase Your Income & Savings

There are numerous opportunities to increase your income and grow your savings. Let's explore some of them.

Making more money

Tip: Begin Earning More

Increase your income by changing jobs, getting a promotion or learning new skills. Lots of people are stuck. It isn't easy to change, that's why so many are stuck in their comfort zone, and not living up to their potential. You know what to do! I can't tell you. But I can say you owe it to yourself and your family to do better, make more money, improve your career, and your standard of living. Sometimes changing careers is the right decision. You may have to go back to school, have a longer commute, or even relocate. The point is, don't settle! Get out there and compete effectively in the economic world.

Despite the current employment situation you still may be able to find part-time employment. I did just that for over twenty years. At one point I was working full time, was a full-time student, employed at a part-time position, and had an active consulting practice. Agreed, everyone's not as loco as I was, but you can gain some extra cash by work-ing an extra job.

Tip: Go to the Job

When it comes to employment, all cities and areas of the country are not equal. There may be opportunities in one place that aren't present in another. You may need to: Go to the job! This means you might have to move or change. "Go to the job," has two meanings: 1) go to the location where the most, and best jobs are available; 2) go into the career field with the most opportunities for employment, advancement, and good compensation. Sure, it may be diffi-cult, but your financial survival could be on the line.

Employer sponsored Plans

If you are fortunate to be employed, be sure to contribute to your employer's 401k, 457k, 403k, or whatever tax-deductible investment or savings plan(s) may be available to you, particularly if there is an employer "match." It's like free $$$.

Tip: Always Contribute Enough to Get the "Match"

Employers will often "match" the employee's contribution to retirement and savings plans. Don't miss out on this chance to get "free money" from your employer!

I've met a number of employees who don't enroll or contribute to these programs and I want to *shake* them. Who, in their right mind would turn down an offer to double their money? So make sure you're enrolled and contribute.

Other money generating options include:

--Opening a business, internet based or otherwise.

--Creating an *IRA* or *SEP.*

--Investing in stocks or bonds.

--buying rental real estate.

--renting out a room in your home.

--turning your hobby into cash.

Although buying stocks or other securities entails risk, in the past it has been a good way to accumulate wealth. Most individuals prefer mutual funds because they offer diversification, professional asset management and comparative safety.

Tip: Consider Foreign Investments

If you could have invested in U.S. stocks eighty years ago think of what a great investment you would have made. Well, you may have a similar opportunity in foreign countries some of which appear to be at the same stage of development today as we were at that time. Consider *ADR*'s (shares of non-U.S. companies traded in U.S. exchanges).
Try www.stocksabroad.com for more information on these investments.

Tip: Take a Risk!

Yes, that's right you should take risk! Just not too much. Greater risk can result in greater profit, but also greater chance for loss. When you're younger you can afford more risk, as time is on your side. As you age you should have more of your assets in "safe investments," like CD's and bonds. A simple formula is: 100 minus your age. By this guideline you should have 30% in "safe" investments when you are 30 – while the remainder can be in stocks. And 60% when you are age 60 with only 40% at risk. Of course this is only a guideline as it ultimately depends on your particular appetite for, and tolerance of, risk.

A 2010 *T. Rowe Price* study confirms the importance of risk-taking. The study examined investment returns from 1950 through the end of 2009 for 10, 20 and 30 year periods. The results revealed that when held for 30 or 20 years an age-appropriate diversified portfolio always beat inflation. And over a ten year holding period it bested the inflation rate 80% of the time. *Price* advocates a higher risk portfolio than the above formula, as under no scenario did investors lose money when investments were held for a minimum of ten years (although the worst 10 tears only returned 1.9%). *www.troweprice.com*

You should vow to increase your income and set aside significant savings. An excellent philosophy is to **"pay yourself first!"** Ten percent should be your minimum goal. More if you can afford it. Your #1 bill each month should be to pay yourself. Yes, your other bills are important but your future wealth accumulation is top priority. You will be amazed at the difference this system will make over a lifetime.

Tip: The Rule of 72

A simple trick will allow you to calculate the approximate time required for money to double at a certain interest rate. The Rule of 72 requires that you divide the interest into 72. For example at 12%, 72 divided by 12 = 6 years. Or at 3% it will take 24 years. (72 divided by 3 = 24). As you can see interest rate is very important - whether you're paying or saving.

Saving only $2,000 a year @ 10% interest will result in a nice little nest egg of over $35,000 in ten years. Or if you have $100 a month to invest at an 8% rate, and keep investing for 30 years, you would end up with over $150,000. *Albert Einstein* half-jokingly called compound interest the "most powerful force in the universe." This is the "magic" of compound interest.

There are so many options when it comes to savings and investments that it can numb the mind, and overwhelm the senses.

Just like I don't want to see you practice careless spending I'd hate to see you lose your hard earned savings in some speculative or otherwise risky investment.

Tip: Prepare for Non-Retirement

The reality of the 21st Century is that many employees and small business owners will have to work until they die. This new era of *non-retirement* may be painful disillusionment for many, but we should have seen it coming. For years now the private sector has been dismantling *"defined benefit plans."* These plans guaranteed a fixed monthly pension amount for the lifetime of the retiree. The new plans put the risk on the employee and include 401k's, stock purchase plans, IRA's, etc. Even the venerable Social Security Retirement plan is under attack and will undoubtedly see more reductions. So either prepare for *non-retirement* or start contributing "'til it hurts" into all available retirement options.

Whether you have a retirement plan or not, you need to start saving! And you can't count on permanent employment. Although you may never be able to retire, that doesn't mean you'll have a job that you like. In fact, *Associated Press, (Washington, Jan. 5, 2010)* reports that "only 45% of Americans are satisfied with their job." And, according to a U.S. Job Recovery and Retention Survey conducted by the *Society for Human Resource Management* a whopping seventy-five percent of all employees are looking for new jobs! An even higher number – 98% - of Americans polled by *Monster.com* and *Hotjobs.com* are "looking to change jobs" in 2011 (Kristina Cooke, *Reuters*, Jan. 21, 2011).

The Company Men

A recent movie, *The Company Men (The Weinstein Company, 2011) starring Ben Affleck, Chis Cooper, Tommy Lee Jones, Kevin Costner, Maria Bello, Rosemarie DeWitt...* depicts the impact of corporate downsizing on employees and their families. These are executive types, affluent, high income execs with lifestyles to match. It's not a new story, *"Death of a Salesman," Arthur Miller's* famous play was produced over 60 years ago, but the loss of a job is just as devastating, and economic circumstances are even more precarious. In the current film, everyone is living at, or above, their considerable means. There are lessons to be learned: misplaced values, build options, live below your means, don't count on job security, family is important, save for emergencies, you are not defined by your job...

High on your priorities must be the accumulation of a substantial reserve. More likely than not, you will need a "cushion." Even if you have stable employment, it's necessary to plan for retirement. There are many investment and savings options to consider. In fact, so many that you will probably need competent, objective, dispassionate, professional help (see Chapter 5).

INVESTMENT & SAVINGS

Here are a few investment and savings options to consider:

Savings Accounts – safe, short term savings, readily available but extremely low returns, most common way to save.

High Yield Bank Accounts – high may be too optimistic, but ready access to funds, and safety.

Money Market Accounts – minimum balance, liquid and accessible, high safety.

CD's – popular, Certificates of Deposit which must be held for a period of months or years, very safe, low returns at this time.

Bonds – various types, U.S. securities, tax-free municipals, state, county, etc. quite safe, U.S. bonds considered completely safe – also consider corporate bonds, inflation-indexed bonds and bond funds.

Mutual Funds – popular, safer than individual stocks, professionally managed, (no-load preferable to load [commission]).

Stocks – individual stocks offer potentially high returns at greater risk, generally liquid. Whereas "Penny stocks" and OTC (over the counter) and some foreign equities typically = much more risk.

Commodities – silver, gold, copper, wheat, corn, etc. are all traded and carry a high level of risk, best left to professionals, (although see tip on following pages).

Note: *There are many more investment and savings instruments and "vehicles" you are advised to consult with a professional before making investment decisions.*

Most investors do not have a good understanding of the intricacies of many financial instruments. As we all learned in the housing debacle, our mortgages were "packaged" by Wall Street types, and sold throughout the known world as *collateralized debt obligations* which were rated much higher than was reflective of their true (marginal value). Sophisticated investors throughout the world were bamboozled by these esoteric cleverly packaged "investments." And took huge losses.

Tip: Good Investments are Elusive

What is a good investment in the early 21st century? Who knows? Is real estate? Are stocks, mutual funds or bonds? Commodities? Accepted wisdom in the 20th century was "buy and hold." If you practiced that advice today you'd likely be a big loser. Foreign stocks in fast growing economies seem attractive. But you have to be careful because their financial regulations are not as stringent. And as we've all discovered, even U.S. regulations don't provide that much protection. Best advice: Educate yourself. Participate in your employee sponsored plans. Find a reputable, trustworthy advisor. And personally monitor the heck out of whatever investments you make.

Beware of crooks

There are many people out there who want to take your money without having your best interests at heart, even supposedly reputable brokers like the infamous *Bernie Madoff* who turned out to be nothing more than a scumbag fraudster. Lesson to the wise: Be careful when making investments!

Tip: Avoid Investment Scams

--No risk or low risk investments with high returns generally do not exist – don't buy it.

--Avoid internet, phone or mail investment solicitations.

--Run away fast if you're asked to keep the investment a secret!

--Avoid plans that require you to recruit other investors.

--Don't deal with unregistered investments or unlicensed salesmen.

--Make sure investments are clearly explained and well documented.

--Limited availability, immediate decisions, and pressure are all "red flags."

--be skeptical about any investment; read all disclosures, ask questions, get other opinions, check reputations and past performance, take your time, and don't be suckered in by some shyster's glowing promises.

Wage earners in their 30's and 40's should be saving at least 15% of their income for emergency reserve and wealth accumulation. Just say: "Yes, I can!" Then do it. You don't have to thank me now, but in retirement you will – if I'm still around...

The array of investments is extensive and you should consider a range of possibilities.

Tip: Income Property

A common investment for many families is income property. There are multiple attractions to residential income property and undoubtedly lots of headaches, too. At the end of the 20th century and the beginning of this one, real estate prices were appreciating so rapidly that "flipping," or short term holding of properties and quick resale, typically following rehab/renovation was very popular. And "investors" made lots of money. However the days of rapid appreciation and easy mortgage money are over. I still like residential income property and own some. Of course you now have to be in it for the long term. It still is attractive for the tax advantages (mortgage deductibility, depreciation, etc.) and perhaps appreciation in value over the long term. Some people start with a duplex or triplex and live in one of the units. If you're handy with repairs and can deal with tenants this may be a good investment. Buy at the low end so that you will be able to cover repair costs or when tenants move out or have to be evicted.

You may even consider renting a room, or larger portion of your house, to offset some of your housing costs and gain a little extra income. Just be careful; screen prospective tenants thoroughly.

There are many simple approaches to saving and investing: savings accounts, *IRA*'s, company retirement plans, etc. More possibilities include: Real Estate investments through

REIT's (real estate investment trust funds), direct real estate investments, even art or other collectibles.

Most Americans dabble in the stock market indirectly through mutual funds or their employer sponsored plans. Some invest in *DRIP*'s (*Dividend Reinvestment Plan*) by buying directly from sponsoring corporations, commission free.

You definitely need to do your homework when investing today. Interest rates at the time this book was written were in the 1-3% range, the stock market was completely unpredictable, real estate values were still declining, and small businesses were in rough shape. Despite this you still need to invest. You've worked for your money and it's necessary to put your money to work for you! Of course precious metals (especially gold), other commodities, (oil particularly), some currencies are hot! And real estate at depressed levels, stocks at low multiples, etc. are bargains. There are always opportunities, no matter what's going on.

Tip: "Buy & Hold" for One Day!

I came across a peculiar investment strategy that involves purchasing the S&P 500 stock Index at the close of business at the end of each month, and holding your "investment" for one day, i.e., selling at the end of the first trading day of each month. According to a study by Howard Silverblatt, senior index analyst at *Standard and Poor's* this strategy has worked consistently since 1999 and produced 70% (!) more in investment returns than holding over the entire period.

Tip: Invest in Precious Metals?

Precious metals have always had appeal; Gold, Platinum and Silver being the favorites. Even base industrial metals like copper, iron and tin have investment – and speculative – interest. In 2008, when the debt crisis emerged the precious metals began a prolonged price rally. Some say this is a speculative bubble, one fueled by banking and currency crises and general economic uncertainty. However, the emerging economies, particularly China and India are experiencing demand resulting from their rapidly expanding wealth. Some nations are even increasing their strategic reserves.

Precious metals, particularly gold, have been a "safe haven" for a thousand years. You may want to consider these commodities in your portfolio. There are many ways to invest; *ETF*'s are popular. These *Exchange Traded Funds* are traded daily on the world's stock exchanges, so they provide liquidity and convenience. However, some Investors like gold mining stocks like *Barrick*, *Newmont Mining* or *GoldCorp* for the leverage they provide, while others want to take possession of the metals in the form of coins or bars.

I like gold and silver, although I prefer the pre-1933 (unconfiscatable) coins for their collector value and beauty. There are plenty of reputable dealers, and a few unscrupulous ones. Do your research. A small stash of gold coins or silver dollars may be just the trick to make you feel more secure!

Tip: The Number

There are books, articles and television commercials about "the number." This is the amount you will need to retire "comfortably." It includes social security, savings, and pension (if any). It is intended that you will never outlive your money. One simple calculation is to determine 75% of your pre-retirement income, and multiply it by 15 to 25. For example you make $40,000 now – you will need $1,000,000 – one million- (25 x $40k) to retire at an equivalent level. For minimal living it would be 15 x $40,000, or $600,000. This means at the top level you would have $40,000 per year, and at the minimal level your retirement income would be $24,000/yr. Scary, isn't it!

Taxes

One more important area which can save you money: You may be paying too much in income taxes. Yes, you! Many taxpayers overpay as a result of ignorance or inattention. A tax professional may save you a small fortune by finding overlooked or esoteric deductions or credits, even more favorable treatment of income, or shifting income or expenses to another year.

Tip: Save $$$ on Income Tax

There are lots of ways to save money on taxes. Be sure to deduct your mortgage interest, student loan interest, refinance "points," home buyer credits, property taxes, charitable donations, certain business expenses, state sales tax, state income tax, stock losses, moving expenses for a new job, child care credit, dependents, casualty and disaster loses, sales tax on new vehicles, energy credits for home improvements, etc., etc. As you can see, there are so many deductions (and I've only listed a few), that you probably are better off filing the long form.

For some filers the 1040ez may work, but it's not advantageous for many. The standard deduction at this time is $5,700 for a single person, $11,400 for a joint return.

While commercial tax filing software could be suitable for your situation, tax preparation is as much an art as it is accounting science. I recommend that you visit a tax professional. You might be surprised at how much you can save.

Insurance

When you spend all this time and effort saving money and making investments to provide financial security, you don't want to see it vanish due to some unfortunate twist of fate. This is where insurance comes in.

Tip: Buy Insurance

Insurance is designed to prevent you from experiencing financial loss – for a price! Should you have insurance? – YES. Should you protect everything against every possible catastrophe? – NO. First, you should cover the major risks in your life. The ones that you couldn't afford to replace. Generally this would include your life, health, your home and vehicle(s). Health insurance is essential because of the risk of incurring major medical costs. (You may also want to buy disability insurance.) Your mortgagor will require that you insure your home, and likewise, your state will require that you carry liability insurance for your vehicle. You will need these coverages, but you don't need to buy extended warranties on automobiles or appliances, eyeglasses or contacts, etc. (Usually manufacturer's product warranties cover you for a minimum of one year.)

Employers frequently provide life, health and disability insurance to employees at a reduced cost. Some even have arrangements for auto or home insurance. This is generally a good option. Be sure to comparison shop – as I pointed out in the prior discussion on auto insurance.

You can save money by choosing higher deductibles, if you can afford the loss. Remember, it's a game of chance. They're betting you won't have a loss, you're thinking that you might. They know the odds, you don't!

This review of investments, taxes and insurance has only scratched the surface. As you are undoubtedly aware, there are plenty of experts available in each of these specialties, and you will need their expertise. Life is increasingly complicated; laws, requirements and regulations frequently change. Financial conditions can turn on a dime. Investment options, conditions, vehicles and instruments are constantly evolving. Your job is to understand what you can to be a savvy investor and competent financially.

Education: a major differentiator

You are, in some ways, an economic machine, living in a financially demanding environment. And, as an economic "machine" you must be efficient, effective, and powerful. One way to increase your value in this economic setting is to have the skills, knowledge, experience and education that places you in demand.

We are a sophisticated society which requires a level of proficiency not easily attained in the K-12 public education system. Admittedly, there are plenty of successful people with a high school education, or less. And, you could be one of those. However, to improve your odds in our economic system my advice is to get more education. Sure I'm biased! As a college and university instructor for the past, well, let's say over twenty years, I understand the relationship between more education and more money.

For much of the past century there were lots of skilled and semi-skilled jobs paying a solid middle-class wage. We were a manufacturing economy, with strong unions like the *Teamsters*, *AFL-CIO*, *Longshoremen*, etc. Things have changed. Now, we're primarily a service-based, technological, information oriented economy that values, and often requires, highly trained and well-educated employees and managers. If you're not already one of these in-demand types, you should consider upping your credentials.

As this book is being written the unemployment rate is dangerously close to 10%, and in some areas even higher. Interestingly there is one category where unemployment is less than half that - those with a four, or more, year college education! This relationship between education and unemployment, and education and earnings is undeniable.

The following chart dramatically demonstrates the value of education. The average person with a bachelor's degree makes two and one-half times as much as those with less than a H.S. diploma. And, the average master's degree holder makes almost triple. The average 4 year college grad makes over twice as much as a high school graduate.

Practically 15% of all those with less than a high school diploma are unemployed, whereas only about 2% of those with a professional degree are. An amazing 700% difference!

Education pays

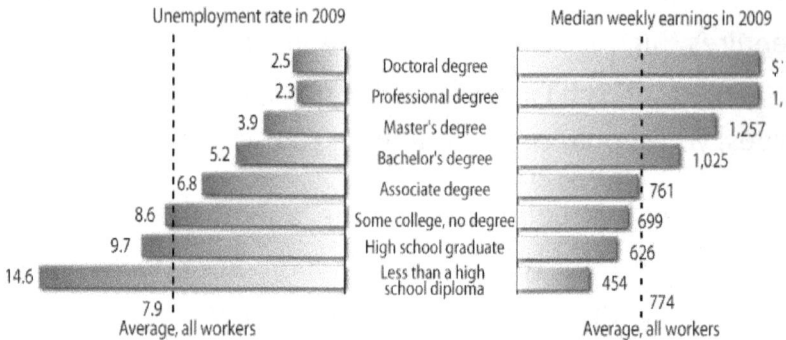

Unemployment rate in 2009		Median weekly earnings in 2009
2.5	Doctoral degree	$
2.3	Professional degree	1,
3.9	Master's degree	1,257
5.2	Bachelor's degree	1,025
6.8	Associate degree	761
8.6	Some college, no degree	699
9.7	High school graduate	626
14.6	Less than a high school diploma	454
7.9 Average, all workers		774 Average, all workers

Source: Bureau of Labor Statistics, Current Population Survey

Source: Bureau of Labor Statistics, *bls.gov/emp*

As attractive as education is as a path to personal growth and financial security, the financing of higher education has become a nightmare for many. High on your list of considerations when selecting a college should be the cost of tuition. Student loans are non-dischargeable through bankruptcy, and may stay with you for a lifetime. And, with job prospects less certain than in the past, there's no guarantee that you will land a position that will enable you to pay your student debt quickly and easily.

So, unless money is not a problem your choice of a college should be partially based on cost. Generally public colleges and universities have significantly lower tuition than private colleges. And, for-profit schools are typically the highest. Make your decision carefully, you don't want to be saddled with a lifetime of debt, or a credit record tainted by a student loan default.

Tip: Think Like an Immigrant

I'm not sure who came up with this phrase, but it certainly applies. (There is a book titled *Immigrant, Inc.*, by Richard Herman and Robert Smith).

Immigrants come to this country with a willingness to work hard and sacrifice. They immediately recognize the opportunities in business and education. They aren't generally as risk-aversive, as those of us who were born here. They believe in the American Dream. Immigrants are over-represented among top founding entrepreneurs. Thinking like an immigrant could open your mind, and help you succeed.

Summary

You are the master of your own destiny. You need to take charge. If you are under-educated or your skills need updating, go back to school and learn a profession or trade. If you're employed become a top employee and try to get promoted. If you don't have enough savings, reduce your expenses and start saving more. If you have no plan for the future, start setting some goals. If you are not invested or your profile is too risky or too conservative for your age and ambition, modify your portfolio.

Begin thinking like the economic entity you are. And behave in a fashion consistent with your financial goals.

Resist the marketers, advertisers, and conspicuous consumption mentality of our society. Your survival is at stake.

University of Connecticut graduation (courant.com)

CHAPTER

5

CHOOSING FINANCIAL EXPERTS

(BY KRZYSZTOF BRYNIUK, MBA, MAC, MM, MED, PA)

We live by the Golden Rule. Those who have the gold make the rules.

~Buzzie Bavasi

Money often costs too much.

~Ralph Waldo Emerson

I'd like to live as a poor man with lots of money.

~Pablo Picasso

When it is a question of money, everybody is of the same religion.

~Voltaire

O Gold! I still prefer thee unto paper,
Which makes bank credit like a bark of vapour.

~Lord Byron

NOTE: *Your financial success and future will undoubtedly depend on the decisions you make. Stop a moment and think. Do you have the expertise it takes to make these decisions? Sure, you can handle the obvious ones, and yes you may have garnered knowledge in this book that will help you. However, the complexities of tax laws, real estate laws, banking laws, investment rules, estate planning, etc., can stymie even the most sophisticated layperson. This is when professional help becomes essential. My colleague, Krzyszstof Bryniuk is a seasoned expert practitioner who teaches college level accounting and finance, and is CEO of Bryniuk & Company, a Miami Accounting firm. I'm sure that you will find his valuable advice cogent, considered, and practical. BAC.*

Good advice- you know, the kind that's helpful,
but hard to follow, is readily available.
If it's difficult and painful it's probably beneficial too.

Dr. Ben

Choosing Financial Experts

by Krzysztof Bryniuk

It is important to have expert advice in managing your money whether you're purchasing a home, investing for retirement, preparing your income tax return, doing estate planning, or involved in a lawsuit. Expert resources can help you successfully navigate the treacherous financial waters in many areas of your life.

Accountant

An accountant can help you manage your expenses, increase your income and save on taxes. If you have a business an accountant can maintain "the books," so that you are making a profit, controlling costs, managing a payroll, and can comply with local, state and federal taxes and regulations.

People generally use accounting services for income tax preparation. While taxpayers may be satisfied with an "income tax preparer" they may not realize that many of these preparers are poorly trained and unknowledgeable.

Accountants come in several categories and with various specialties. A *CPA* is a *Certified Public Accountant* who has passed a rigorous examination and has necessary credentials and education. The CPA is licensed by the State and certified to meet all requirements and standards. A *Public*

Accountant is another designation which is gradually being phased out.

A *CPA* will be capable of handling a wide range of areas of finance: estate planning, financial planning, financial analysis, forensic accounting, tax accounting, corporate finance, etc. However it may be preferable to work with a specialist, particularly for complicated financial matters.

How do you find a competent accountant? The best way is from a personal referral. If a friend or professional colleague can vouch for the competence, integrity, and professionalism of the accountant that's the best recommendation. If you don't have a referral, call accountants in your area, and be sure to have a face-to-face meeting before deciding.

Please note: If it's a tax matter, an *Enrolled Agent*, licensed by the *IRS*, may be your best choice, particularly for audits, tax collection demands, or complex tax problems.

Attorney / Lawyer

Attorneys are law school graduates who have passed the Bar examination for the state in which they practice law. You may need to hire an attorney to consult with or represent you in contractual matters, divorce, business or estate matters, if you are charged with a crime, or a party to a lawsuit. Attorneys do not generally charge for the first meeting. This meeting is necessary for both participants to clarify the legal matter, decide whether representation is required and gain a preliminary under-standing of issues, process, costs, and timeframes.

Real Estate Professional

A Real Estate Broker or Agent can be a valuable resource in buying or selling properties, escrow, or ownership matters, property valuations and negotiations. Not all real estate agents or brokers are *Realtors* who belong to the *National Association of Realtors* and pledge to conduct business by their standards and code of ethics. All Real Estate agents are licensed by the state after passing a Real Estate exami-nation.

Real Estate agents are typically located through referrals. Ask your friends or work colleagues to make recommenda-tions. Also look for *For Sale* signs in your neighborhood to see who has the most listings. Pay particular attention to the *Sold* signs to determine which agent is most successful in concluding transactions.

Financial Planner

Look for a *Certified Financial Planner* or a *Chartered Finan-cial Planner.* These designations are legitimate and unfortunately anyone can call themselves a "financial planner" and some are dishonest or fraudulent. Get refer-rals from friends or associates. You can also search databases for listings of agents in your area. The best are the *National Association of Personal Financial Advisors,* and the *Financial Planning Association.* Be sure to verify credentials, although even solid credentials do not guarantee honesty.

Financial Planners are paid for their services by fee or commissions, or a combination. Fee charges can either be asset-based, fixed or hourly. Hourly fees are typically from $100 to $400, and this is generally the best, most cost-effective arrangement.

Meet with several candidates and select the one who seems to best reflect your investment and retirement philosophy. Get all agreements in writing.

Stockbroker

To purchase stock you must have a *stockbroker.* A stockbroker is a salesperson who works for a *brokerage house (e.g., Merrill Lynch, Charles Schwab, Scottrade, E-Trade, Morgan-Stanley, etc.)*

Stockbrokers must pass licensing examinations before they are permitted to execute transactions (buy or sell) shares for you on the exchanges.

Full service brokers offer a wide range of services such as stocks, bonds, annuities, insurance, or derivatives. They are almost always paid by commission, based on account activity. *Discount brokers* don't offer advice or research but charge considerably less. Often their fees are nominal fixed charges per transaction.

Compare services, fees, and minimum account require-ments on-line. Ask friends and colleagues who they use.

Banker

It's important to have a relationship with your bank or cre-dit union. Over the years these relationships have changed with more and more transactions being done on-line or at *ATM* machines. With these technologies, fewer people than ever even need to visit a bank. The most important relationship with your bank becomes one of paying your bills on time, avoiding overdrawing your accounts, and perhaps getting a line of credit, home improvement or other loan. Etc.

Business owners generally prefer smaller, local institutions so that they can establish a more personal relationship with their banker. This relationship will be useful if a loan is needed.

Insurance Agent

You need to protect your assets and *an Insurance Agent* can help you do this. Insurance agents are licensed (by the State) to sell insurance and related products. Sometimes they act as financial advisors and may offer mutual funds, annuities, etc. You will want to have homeowners insur-ance, casualty, life, disability, automobile insurance, etc. With the advent of low cost insurers, discounters, specia-lized agents, and the increasing Internet presence, you have more options than ever. Ask your friends and business colleagues for reference, and comparison shop on line. A good agent may be able to save you money, give you peace of mind, and bundle coverages to simplify your insurance and reduce costs.

Finding the Right One

Financial experts can have a major impact on your life. They can help you find financial security or worsen your prospects. Be careful in choosing who to hire.

Practice "CCT" in selecting your advisors. You should be **C**omfortable, **C**onfident and have **T**rust in the expert(s) you decide to do business with. You have to be comfortable in discussing personal financial matters, confident that the expert is knowledgeable and qualified, and trust that the expert will provide objective, sound, and honest advice, consistent with your best interests.

CHAPTER

6

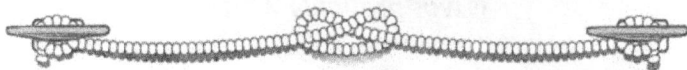

CONCLUSION

It is an unfortunate human failing that a full pocketbook often groans more loudly than an empty stomach.

~Franklin Delano Roosevelt

Inflation is when you pay fifteen dollars for the ten-dollar haircut you used to get for five dollars when you had hair.

~Sam Ewing

Business is the art of extracting money from another man's pocket without resorting to violence.

~Max Amsterdam

If you lend someone $20, and never see that person again, it was probably worth it.

~Anonymous

Lack of money is the root of all evil.

~George Bernard Shaw

CONCLUSION

You're almost done, but you're not off the hook yet. I'm not sure you're sufficiently uncomfortable or motivated to take action. Immediate action! Not next week, next month or next year. If I'm right, and you're not, here's your last chance! Go back to chapter one and earnestly reconsider your relationship with money and see if any of the behaviors and attitudes describe you. Return to chapter two and complete your *Budget* and *Net Worth* statements. Look at these worksheets and see where you're out of line. Make a spending plan that will permit you to pay your bills and have money left over each month for savings, investment, and pleasure.

Review chapters three and four and see what applies. Trim unnecessary expenses, manage your money better, and plan for the future. Seriously consider your options. I've tried to emphasize the importance of not ruling out major lifestyle changes. But it's all up to you.

If you're in over your head and need professional assistance, re-read *Professor Bryniuk's* chapter on Choosing Financial Experts. Often it's best to get professional advice; this is particularly true when it comes to business, investments, tax, divorce, and bankruptcy matters.

By now you have figured out that there are actions you can take, and changes you can make. My college economics professor (refer to Appendix) is not completely correct. His path to riches: "born rich, marry rich, or be lucky and smart" does not tell the whole story. There are many Americans who achieve financial security by a more common approach. The formula I have in mind is: 1) live below your means, 2) save your money, 3) invest your savings, and 4) make more money.

So if there aren't any eligible rich marriage prospects for you, and you were not born rich and you're not all that lucky, you can still be smart and disciplined and end up financially successful and secure.

Perhaps you're already wealthy and are merely reading this book for amusement. If so, you can still walk away with something. Even the most affluent like to generate a little extra income, and save some cash. Sometimes these wealthy individuals are the biggest financial conservatives of all. Even if you find one useful tip you're better off. Take what you can from this book.

My message is not about austerity and denial, it's more about self-control and responsibility. It's about putting yourself in charge of your life and your destiny. Empowerment is heady, it can foster confidence and optimism. Small steps and steady financial progress will sustain you.

I've tried to make this book fun, not only to hold your interest but to defuse some of the anxiety surrounding this intensely personal and emotional subject. I purposely did not go into great depth about many financial instruments and options. I certainly didn't want you to feel overwhelmed, or worse yet give up because of the complexities. And there are specialists in each area of financial decision-making. Seek up-to-date, professional advice when confronted with important decisions.

To reiterate, my main objective was to get you interested in ascertaining your current financial status and to become motivated to improve that condition. There is always room for further study and consultation with experts, when you're ready. Ultimately it takes your willingness and initiative to make changes and the discipline to implement them and follow through.

We're going through a major worldwide economic shift. There's a huge transfer of wealth from the U.S. and other developed countries to developing nations, this ultimately means a further erosion of our standard of living. The primary beneficiaries are the brick countries --- that's spelled *BRIC*. *BRIC* stands for *Brazil, Russia, India and China*. These nations have some of the fastest growing economies in the world. Certainly they're the dominant ones. They're getting wealthy primarily at our expense. It's not their fault; nations have done this throughout history. And eventually they may get fat, sassy and complacent, too.

In this economic realignment the U.S. has slipped to number 10 (*CIA World Factbook*, 2010) in Gross Domestic Product *per capita* (on a purchasing power parity basis). Essentially, this is a calculation of purchasing power and standard of living. The highest countries are: *Qatar* at $145,300, tiny *Lichtenstein* with over $120,000 annually, and prosperous nations like *Luxembourg* and *Bermuda*. *Norway*, *Kuwait*, and *Singapore* also boast higher per capita income. But the real up-and-comers are those *BRIC* countries although they have a long way to go to catch up.

So as a nation we're falling behind in rate of economic growth, individual income, and standard of living. And, although we're still quite prosperous, the trend is ominous. We're presently engaged in a huge *Ponzi*-like scheme wherein we're shifting enormous amounts of debt to foreign countries and future generations of Americans. Efforts directed at bringing this practice under control are likely to fail.

This economic turmoil may take years to play out. Or we may get rapid swings or changes. Volatility is increasing, and we're in a confusing, unpredictable environment. If you trust in linear, predictable, slow moving, stable financial and economic conditions, you're in for further "shock and awe."

You see how quickly things can change. You survived the greatest economic downturn since the *Great Depression*. You coped with around 10% unemployment. You witnessed the default of previously thought stable *European Union* countries. You were buffeted by the greatest housing and mortgage crisis we've seen. You've seen the once *almighty dollar* decline in value and questioned as a world *reserve currency*. You've experienced skyrocketing commodities prices including food, oil, and gold. You've watched the prestige and strength of the *United States* erode, and you've seen our leaders struggle with an overwhelming debt problem. You've seen many major companies, merchandisers and small businesses close. You've witnessed credit availability almost completely evaporate. You've seen multi-trillion dollar deficits and bailouts. Your sense of security and confidence in the future has been rocked. And all of this occurred in the first decade of the 21st century!

I'm not an alarmist, a survivalist, or a "gloom and doomer." But I do believe that the profound disarray in our economy is cause for a prudent response, and another compelling reason to look after your financial stability. I wholeheartedly encourage you to take the initiative to improve your finances.

So start planning. Armed with data about your true financial situation examine your personality, relationship with money, and perhaps self-defeating beliefs and behaviors. Vow to change. Understand the urgency as things continue to deteriorate. Reject the marketing, consumer-driven attitudes that define our society. Success is not what they're selling.

Make a commitment to yourself to reduce your dependence on the corporate, government, and economic system. Be more aware of the precarious nature of your personal finances and endeavor to increase your financial reserves. Set personal financial goals and measure your progress in attaining them. Know your net worth like you know your birthdate or social security number. None of this is easy. If you want to be a financial survivor you must be determined, resourceful, resilient, and self-reliant.

You can hope that things improve. You can believe that our leaders will solve the current economic dilemma. You can think that some revolutionary idea will change everything. But what if it doesn't happen? Do you want to be a pawn all of your life? Or do you want to take charge of your life; your finances, and your destiny?

These are questions only you can answer. And there are actions only you can take.

When it comes to money, enough for survival is the first step.
Once that's been accomplished, you can't rest.
Then it's on to accumulation of more for a secure future and
further acquisition of life's pleasures.

Dr. Ben

APPENDIX

CAN YOU GET RICH?

Thrift comes too late when you find it at the bottom of your purse.

~Seneca

If you think nobody cares if you're alive, try missing a couple of car payments.

~Earl Wilson

Note: This is an article I wrote, published in 2008, and included in my previous book, ***Bites of Business.*** It is clearly applicable here as well.

Let's Get Rich!

My undergraduate economics professor insightfully said: "There are three ways to get rich in America: 1) Be born Rich, 2) Marry rich, or 3) Be awfully lucky or very smart." He went on to say: "For most of us, by far the easiest way is to "marry rich, and that's what I did!"

Most of my Business students want to know how to get rich. After all, that's why some of them study business. In this country "bigger is better" and that includes bank accounts. People want more of everything – especially money. Many authors have made tidy sums writing books about getting wealthy. It's a very popular subject.

The book *"Rich Dad, Poor Dad,"* (Robert Kiyosaki & Sharon Lechter, 2001) emphasizes knowledge, experience, and attitude. This information is useful and sound. The Rich Dad mindset touts investments before consumption. But we are a nation of consumers, and 70% of our GNP is based on consumer spending, so spending money (often unnecessarily) is almost a national pastime.

Suze Orman, internationally acclaimed financial advisor, has a TV show (CNBC) where she consistently emphasizes "financial responsibility." She believes that Americans (especially women) have a "totally dysfunctional" relationship with money (Time, CNN, April 5, 2007).

What is the secret to becoming rich? Well, if I knew I'd be there. And, the authors of "Money" magazine(s), books, newsletters, etc., can't tell you either. You see, wealth is as much a state of mind as anything. Like anything else, it's all a matter of perspective. And, there is not a handy roadmap with clear directions to your wealth destination.

Is there a Science for Getting Rich?

In his book *"The Science of Getting Rich"* (2001 ed., orig. pub. 1910) William Wattles tries to make a case for a "scientific" approach to becoming wealthy. His theory is built upon "financial success through creative thought," and the interconnectedness of all elements in the universe, including thoughts. The use of mental imagery and vision are cornerstones of the approach. The premise is that if the vision is strong enough the universe will conspire to develop a realization of the subject of the thought, i.e., $$$$. Wattle's book is claimed to be a precursor to the wildly popular *"The Secret"* (movie [2006], and book [2007]).

The Secret refers to the "Law of Attraction" which insists that you will attract what you think about most. Interestingly, a "down on his luck" lottery player earning about "$300 a week" practiced this method concentrating on money, and in 2007 won a Florida Lottery prize of $33 million (*Miami Herald*, Aug. 8, 2007). Draw your own conclusions.

Luck, Hard Work, Intelligence

Many people think rich folk are smarter or work harder than the rest of us. And, oftentimes that's true. However, many of the hardest workers are not rich, and most of the smartest people aren't either. So, what is the explanation? Obviously, the secret to becoming rich does not depend so much on these attributes as it does on some other factor(s).

How about "luck"? Yes indeed, luck does seem to play a role. Choosing the "right" business or career. Living in the "right" area at a fortuitous period. Taking advantage of a "once in a lifetime" opportunity. Or "falling" into a favorable situation. How many people prospered from buying a home or other real estate during a good period? Were they omniscient, or particularly analytical? Usually not. Although some of them recognized a trend and jumped on the bandwagon. However, probably an equal number didn't realize what was going on, or failed to get out before the situation reversed. Much of our wealth can often be attributed to "dumb luck" rather than astuteness.

Obviously, luck seems to play a role in good fortune, misfortune, or amassing a fortune.

Discipline

One of the more data-based studies of wealth involved surveying wealthy individuals. *"The Millionaire Next Door"* (Thomas Stanley & William Danko, 1996) captured attitudes and experiences of wealthy people and found that most had accumulated their riches by being disciplined over the years. The old-fashioned attitudes of thrift, even frugality, spending less than you earn, and long-term goals were in clear evidence in the study.

Preparation

Of course, there is something to be said for preparation. Taking courses, studying, reading books, accumulating information, are all helpful. The old axiom "a fool and his money are soon parted" rings true. Unknowledgeable individuals will make uninformed decisions which have a higher probability of being poor ones. Study and try to become expert in those areas which will enhance your probability of financial success.

Make Getting Rich a Priority

Napoleon Hill wrote what is perhaps the most famous of all wealth books. His *"Think and Grow Rich"* (pub. 1937) described "Laws of Success" including such characteristics as: desire, faith, conquering your fears, and persistence. He recommends "self talk" to reinforce your motivation, attitudes, and commitments.

Just deciding that accumulating wealth is a top priority will help. Accumulating wealth is not necessarily dependent on making more money. Frequently, our investment and spending priorities are the deciding factors. Evaluating your life's priorities to decide what is personally most important is a requisite step. Establishing a top priority necessarily means that other priorities will have to take a subordinate place. And your top priorities will consume most of your attention, time and energy. This may not be exactly what you want, after all. There are tradeoffs and family, personal life, and your desire to lead the so-called "balanced life" may suffer.

Goals, Focus, Effort

Perhaps a more direct, commonplace and business-like approach is called for. People with goals are more likely to succeed. "Goal Theory" indicates that having specific, well-defined goals make us focus on outcomes, direct our energies, and increase our likelihood of attainment. Of course merely wanting to be rich will not result in our becoming wealthy. The goal(s) needs to be "specific," "measurable," "attainable," "realistic," and "timely." These SMART goals, as they are referred to, will significantly improve your odds.

Most people do not have very specific financial goals. As a result, they are easily distracted from their general objective of "getting rich." Also many individuals do not have measurable goals. They have not decided on what wealth actually means to them, and how they will measure it. A simple "net worth" statement, calculating the difference between assets and liabilities should suffice. In order to attain a goal it needs to be reasonably within your reach. There are many millionaires– around 1% of the population (New York Post, June 25, 2008) so attaining that goal seems fairly realistic.

Finally, timeliness includes developing "benchmarks," interim steps and periodically assessing your results. Attaching dates to these interim goals will help you achieve your ultimate goal. And you need sufficient time. If you're eighty years old with $5,000 in total assets your goal is to accumulate $1 million by the time you're eighty-five, although it may be specific and measurable, your goal is not realistic, attainable and TIMELY. On the other hand, if you're twenty-five and have the million dollars net worth goal you have plenty of time, and opportunities to realistically attain it providing you apply the SMART principles.

<u>Getting Rich the SMART way</u>

Maybe getting rich is not so mysterious and elusive after all. It doesn't require having the "right" relatives, super-intelligence, extraordinary luck, or "marrying rich!" It may not even require esoteric, mystical or sacrificial approaches or techniques. Perhaps it's just like any other goal or ambition. What we must do is apply ourselves, and focus on developing a SMART goal. Then comes the essential part, finding the discipline, energy and focus to attain your goal.

To get rich is glorious.

~Deng Xiaoping,
Chinese Statesman
(mid 20th Century)

Money alone sets the world in motion.

~Publilius Syrus,
Roman Slave & Latin Writer
(about 100 B.C.)

Glossary

ADR – American Depository Receipt, represents ownership of shares of a non-U.S. company that trades on American financial markets/stock exchanges

Annuity – an investment that will pay recurring payments, generally for the lifetime of an individual

ASE – a certification for mechanics by the National Institute for Automotive Service Excellence

Asset – an owned economic resource (e.g., bank account, IRA account, home, automobile)

Bad debt – an uncollectable debt

Bailout – generally refers to massive infusion of government money to "save" failing or at risk businesses and financial institutions

Bankruptcy – an insolvent state where a person or company cannot pay their debts

Billionaire – a person whose wealth is $1,000,000,000 or greater

Bond – an obligation (of a government entity or company) with guaranteed repayment obligations

BRIC – acronym representing emerging economies of the following countries: Brazil, Russia, India, and China

Budget – a statement of financial position, with amounts for income and expenses, and balances

Cash Flow – net income after taxes and charges

CD – Certificate of Deposit

CFP – Certified Financial Planner

Conspicuous consumption – wasteful or excessive spending

Cost – the amount paid for something

CPA – Certified Public Accountant

Credit Card – a card authorizing purchases on credit i.e., advancing funds

Debit Card – similar to a credit card, but funds are withdrawn directly from the cardholder's bank account

Debt – money owed

Debtor – a person who owes money

Default – failure to pay according to agreed upon terms

Deficiency Judgment – A court order requiring a debtor to pay the difference between the sales price and the loan balance when the recovery is lower than the outstanding balance (applicable to foreclosures in some States)

Defined Benefit Plan – A retirement plan which provides for specific, unchanging monthly, quarterly, or annual payments to the retiree

Delinquency – late payment or overdue payment on a debt

Diversification – A strategy to reduce risk by requiring investment in a variety of assets instead of one or a few

Downsize – a strategy to reduce expenses frequently includes less costly purchases, a smaller car, and particularly a less expensive residence

DRIP – Dividend Reinvestment Plan, direct investment in a company's stock without commission

Employer match – commitment by an employer to provide an identical amount of payment to an employee's contribution, generally to a savings or investment plan

ETF – Exchange Traded Fund, an investment fund traded on stock exchanges like a stock

Expenses – financial outlays typically as a cost of living or doing business

Expenditures – funds paid

FICO – a score intended to indicate the credit–worthiness of an individual

Financial Infidelity – when a spouse (or significant other) over-spends family money then lies about it or fails to inform their partner

Flip / flipping – purchase of real estate by an investor and rapid resale at a higher price, frequently after only days or months

401 k – a government sponsored retirement savings plan with special tax advantages, similar programs include 403b and 457, etc. (numbers refer to sections of the tax code)

Foreclosure – legal proceeding by a mortgagor to take over a property from a debtor

Income – incoming money; gain

Investment – money directed to a business, property, or security in anticipation of financial gain

IRA – Individual Retirement Account: a retirement savings account, typically with favorable tax treatment – traditional IRA's provide for tax deferred contributions (see Roth IRA)

Land Contract – a "contract for deed," or "installment contract" where the seller provides purchase financing for real property (real estate)

Late payment – a payment made after the due date

Law of Attraction – you receive what you think about, often applied to money and wealth

Liability – an obligation (debt) or account payable

Luxury – a high-end product or service; something adding to comfort over and above necessities

"Match" – contributions made to an employee's retirement account by the employer, in accord with some established formula or agreement

Maxed out – a term describing exhaustion of a credit limit(s) typically on credit card(s)

MBA – Master of Business Administration

Millionaire - a person whose wealth is $1,000,000 or greater

Minimalist – one who keeps spending and/or lifestyle requirements to a minimum

Minimum payment – generally the minimum monthly payment required by a creditor to keep the account in good standing

Money – object(s) exchanged for goods and services; payments

Muni – refers to a Municipal Bond

Net Worth – total assets minus total liabilities

PA – Public accountant

Positive Cash Flow – a condition where income exceeds outgo

Propensity to Consume – an economics term, usually described as MPC (marginal propensity to consume) a formula that explains that increased consumer spending is induced from increased disposable income

Puritan Ethic – rigid morality and ultra-conservative values

Predatory lending – taking advantage of a person with poor credit or desperate need by charging a high interest rate, and/or requiring onerous terms

Rent/Buy decision – a financial decision to decide whether buying a home or renting one is the most financially advantageous

Return – refers to ROI – return on investment

Rent-to-Buy – see *land contract* Note: also refers to arrangements to purchase furniture or appliances; "deals" that should be avoided

REO – Real Estate Owned (property reverts to lender)

Repossession – lender takes back property from a delinquent borrower – usually automobiles

Reverse Mortgage – a Home Equity Conversion Mortgage which allows you to cease mortgage payments and instead receive a portion of your equity paid to you monthly

Rich – an abundance of wealth/possessions/money

Risk – chance for loss, or less than expected return on investment

ROI – return on investment

Roth IRA – a specialized IRA (Individual Retirement Account) with provisions permitting withdrawals not subject to taxation when conditions are met

"Rule of 72" – a technique for roughly calculating investment returns by dividing the rate into the number seventy-two to ascertain how long it takes for the investment to double in value

Savings – money accumulated and held in reserve

Secured – a loan secured by underlying asset(s) or collateral

Short Sale – A Real Estate sale where the sales price is less than the mortgage balance

SMART – a goal setting acronym signifying Specific, Measurable, Attainable, Realistic, and Timely

Solvent – i.e., *financially solvent* able to pay debts

Sticker shock – surprise at the cost of an item, usually an unpleasant reaction

Sub-prime – a borrower or loan to low income or poor credit risk individuals at a higher interest rate

"Underwater"— when you owe more on an asset(s) than it's worth

"Upside-down" -- see "underwater"

Unsecured – debt for which there is no asset pledged as collateral (frequently houses and cars)

Wealth – measure of cash, assets, possessions, etc. with material value

When it comes to finances: desire, impulsivity and greed generally trumps good judgment.

Dr. Ben

BIBLIOGRAPHY

LIST OF REFERENCES

Thrift comes too late when you find it at the bottom of your purse.

~Seneca

Money isn't the most important thing in life, but it's reasonably close to oxygen on the "gotta have it" scale.

~Zig Ziglar

He that wants money, means, and content is without three good friends.

~William Shakespeare

If inflation continues to soar, you're going to have to work like a dog just to live like one.

~George Gobel

In the old days a man who saved money was a miser; nowadays he's a wonder.

~Anonymous

List of References

Alcoholics Anonymous, *www.AA.org*

American Bankruptcy Institute, *www.abiworld.org*

American Cancer Society, *www.cancer.org*

Bankruptcy Abuse and Consumer Protection Act, 2005, *www.bankruptcygov.net*

Bankruptcy Reform Act of 2005, *www.bankruptcy.gov*

Bloomberg, (Personal Finance), *www.bloomberg.com*

Brainy Quote, *www.brainyquote.com*

Byrne, Rhonda, *The Secret,* New York, Atria Books, 2006.

Chilton, David, *The Wealthy Barber*, New York, Prima Pub., 1991.

Consumer Credit Counselors, *www.cccsstl.org*

CNBC, www.CNBC.com

Credit Cards, *www.creditcards.com*

Credit Card Reform Act of 2009, *www.federalreserve.gov*

Credit Union National Association, *www.cuna.org*

Danko, William & Stanley, Thomas J., *The Millionaire Next Door: The Surprising Secrets of America's Wealthy*, Atlanta, Longstreet Press, 1996.

Givens, Charles, *Wealth Without Risk,* New York, Simon Schuster, *1988*

Herman, Richard T, and Smith, Robert L., *Immigrant, Inc.*, New York, Wiley, 2009

Hill, Napoleon, *Think and Grow Rich*, New York, CreateSpace, 1937

Hot Jobs, *www.hotjobs.yahoo.com*

Kipplinger (Financial Advice & Services) *www.kiplinger.com*

Kiyosakl, Robert, *Rich Dad Poor Dad*, New York, Bantam Doubleday, 1999.

Lyman, D., *The Moral Sayings of Publius Syrus*, Cincinnati, 1856

Maslow, Abraham, (1943) "A Theory of Human Motivation," *Psychological Review*, vol. 50, #4, pp.370-396,

Moberg, David "What Vacation Days?" *In These Times*, (June 18, 2007)

Monster, *www.monster.com*

MSN Money, *www.msn.com*

National Park Service, *www.nps.gov*

Opdyke, Jeff, *The Wall Street Journal Complete Personal Finance Guidebook*, New York, Three Rivers Press, 2006.

Quote Garden, *www.quotegarden.com*

Reuters news service, *www.reuters.com*

Robbins, Anthony, *Awaken the Giant Within*, New York, Simon & Schuster, 1991

Sexual Compulsives Anonymous, *www.sca-recovery.org*

Society for Human Resource Management, www.shrm.org

StocksAbroad, *www.stocksabroad.com*

T. Rowe Price, *www.troweprice.com*

The Wall Street Journal, *www.wsj.com*

U.S. Bureau of Labor Statistics, *www.bls.gov*

U.S. Census Bureau, *www.census.gov*

U.S. Department of Labor, *www.dol.gov*

U.S. Internal Revenue Service (IRS), www.irs.gov

U.S. Trustee Program, *www.justice.gov*

Wattles, William, *The Science of Getting Rich*, Whitefish, MT., Kessinger Publishing, 2004 (orig. pub. 1912)

Whitehouse, Mark, *Wall Street Journal "Americans Pare Debt,"* (March 12, 2010)

Yahoo! Finance, *www. finance.yahoo.com*

Credit for images:

p. 41, googleimages
p. 61, jackygalchon.edublogs.org
p. 74, architecture.about.com
p. 127, bigfoto.com – freepicturedownloads
p. 152, courant.com – *Hartford Courant*

A life of luxury requires money. Fame, intelligence, or hard work doesn't guarantee enduring wealth.
It's that other dirty word: Discipline.

Dr. Ben

CONTRIBUTOR

KRZYSZTOF BRYNIUK
(CHAPTER 5)

Krzysztof Bryniuk is a professor of business and applied management, and teaches accounting, finance, international business and economics courses at the undergraduate level. He received a B.S., MEd, and Master of Management from Poznan University of Economics in Europe.

In 2008, Bryniuk earned an MBA from Florida Atlantic University. He continues his studies at the graduate level in the School of Accounting at FAU. Krzysztof Bryniuk is President and CEO of Bryniuk & Company – Accounting Firm.

Professor Bryniuk has extensive experience in real estate, banking, hospitality, accounting and finance. He worked for Bank Slaski, a partner of ING Group, Bank Peako S.A., Unicredit Group, and Miami Dade College. He is an active member of the American Accounting Association.

It's comfortable to have lots of money.
But it's more rewarding to have wealth when you have
purpose.

Dr. Ben

INDEX

Get an education;
and if you don't have money it will at least help you more fully
understand how impoverished you really are.

Then put that education to use for your emotional
and financial benefit.

Dr. Ben

ABOUT
THE AUTHOR

Ben Carlsen

About the Author

Dr. BEN A. CARLSEN, MBA is author of the book *Bites of Business*, and a popular writer of business and finance articles. In *Personal Financial Survival: A Rescue Plan* he tackles the important and timely topic of Personal Finance. He ventured into this area in recognition of the chaotic economy, and its profound impact on practically every-one. Having experienced substantial financial success and major financial reversals in his own life he learned from real-life as well as professionally and academically, and he felt there was a need for practical no-nonsense advice, and a direct explanation of choices and actions.

Carlsen's professional career has been primarily in management: in the public sector, private enterprise and academia. His finance experience includes managing an accounting section, a major Finance Division operation, a disbursements office as a *Principal Fiscal Analyst* for Los Angeles County, and running his own businesses. He gained entirely different perspectives from helping clients budget their household expenses during a stint as a *Social Worker* shortly after graduating from college, and subsequently as a *Real Estate Agent, Tax Preparer* and *Day Trader*.

Dr. Ben, as he's known to his students, earned his Bachelor's Degree at the *University of Washington*, an MBA at *Pepperdine University*, and a Doctorate, majoring in Organization and Leadership, at the *University of San Francisco*. His teaching experience was gained in the business, management, and professional development programs at various institutions of higher learning, including: the *University of San Francisco, University of California (Davis), California State University (Dominguez Hills), Western International University (Phoenix), Axia College (University of Phoenix), and Corinthian Colleges (Miami).* Dr. Carlsen was selected "Teacher of the Year" at the *University of San Francisco*, and "Instructor of the Year" for *Corinthian Colleges*. He's listed in Who's Who of Business Leaders, Who's Who in California, and Who's Who in the World. Throughout his career, Carlsen won numerous awards including the Distinguished Service Award by the *Association for Systems Management*, and a Commendation scroll for innovative leadership from the *Los Angeles County Board of Supervisors*.

When I was young I thought that money was the most important thing in life; now that I am old I know that it is.

~Oscar Wilde

Wouldst thou shut up the avenues of ill,
Pay every debt as if God wrote the bill.

~Ralph Waldo Emerson

Creditors have better memories than debtors.

~Benjamin Franklin

I believe that thrift is essential to well-ordered living.

~John D. Rockefeller

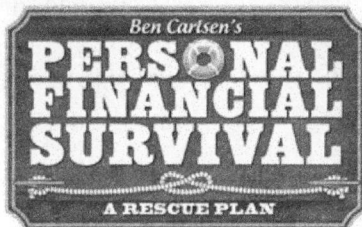

PUBLISHED BY PALM SPRINGS PUBLISHING (2011)
AND

STRATEGIES FOR ASPIRING, NOVICE, &
EXPERIENCED MANAGERS

BY BEN CARLSEN
PUBLISHED BY STANYARD CREEK PUBLISHING (2010)

BOOKS ARE AVAILABLE AT:
AMAZON.COM
AND BOOKSTORES EVERYWHERE

For more information check out my website: bitesofbusiness.com

At this location you will find my blog with tips, strategies, articles, re-sources, etc.

BITES of BUSINESS includes topics related to both your professional busi-ness life and your personal financial business.

www.ingramcontent.com/pod-product-compliance
Lightning Source LLC
LaVergne TN
LVHW011155080426
835508LV00007B/415